D0977154

More Praise for *Make It, Don't Fake It*

"Sabrina shares her insights and wisdom gleaned from years of working with tech executives, venture capitalists, and influencers about how doing the right thing results in the right thing to do. In *Make It, Don't Fake It*, Sabrina shows us that faking it is for losers. Learn how to make it with ethics, passion, confidence, pride, and resilience."
  —Andy Cunningham, Steve Jobs's publicist, bestselling author of *Get to Aha!*, and CEO, Cunningham Collective

"In the 1990s, Sabrina became a valued extension of the PeopleSoft team at a time when core values and beliefs were a novel concept. She kept pace with us as we adapted our core values to navigate PeopleSoft through high growth, bringing a new technology (client/server) to market, and an initial public offering. We could always count on her honesty, candor, and creativity, and, quite simply, we liked and trusted her. This book shows why. She approaches business and life from an integrity-first perspective and 'keeps things real'—a strategy that I believe is fundamental to building successful and enduring products and companies."
  —Dave Duffield, founder of PeopleSoft, Workday, and Ridgeline

"Whether you are a first-time entrepreneur or a seasoned executive, *Make It, Don't Fake It* is an essential guide for leading with purpose and integrity. There are no 'growth hacks' or shortcuts to success. Sabrina delivers a compelling message at a critical time."
  —Jay Fulcher, Chairman and CEO, Zenefits

"This is a no-nonsense, straightforward guide to succeeding in business as well as life. Sabrina's insightful, commonsense approach to success has led her to it time and time again. Her book is a road map from which all can learn and apply to their lives!"
  —David J. Moore, founder, 24/7 Real Media; former President, WPP Digital; Chairman, IAB; and cofounder and CEO, BritePool

"Sabrina Horn's *Make It, Don't Fake It*, loaded with gems of leadership and stories of her personal growth as founder and CEO, is a *required and meaningful primer* for both budding and experienced leaders. Her emphasis on transparency, values, and culture is interwoven throughout. The impact this emphasis had on her decisions when the chips were down or up is as clear a lesson as any leader or CEO should think about and implement. Refreshing to me were the stories of failure, what they meant, and how she rebounded. Her practical advice is first rate and should be taught in business schools everywhere. I've known Sabrina for thirty years, and this book is a marvelous testament to her mission and to her life as a successful businesswoman."

—Ray Rothrock, venture capitalist, board member, CEO, and philanthropist

"Sabrina Horn offers up a pragmatic real-world approach for today's business leaders, which will increase their probability of success in navigating the complex labyrinth that will be required to achieve one's goals."

—Peter Sobiloff, Managing Director, Insight Partners

SABRINA HORN

MAKE IT, DON'T FAKE IT

LEADING WITH AUTHENTICITY FOR REAL BUSINESS SUCCESS

BK

Berrett–Koehler Publishers, Inc.

Copyright © 2021 by Sabrina Horn

All rights reserved. No part of this publication may be reproduced, distributed, or transmitted in any form or by any means, including photocopying, recording, or other electronic or mechanical methods, without the prior written permission of the publisher, except in the case of brief quotations embodied in critical reviews and certain other noncommercial uses permitted by copyright law. For permission requests, write to the publisher, addressed "Attention: Permissions Coordinator," at the address below.

Berrett-Koehler Publishers, Inc.
1333 Broadway, Suite 1000
Oakland, CA 94612-1921
Tel: (510) 817-2277
Fax: (510) 817-2278
www.bkconnection.com

ORDERING INFORMATION
Quantity sales. Special discounts are available on quantity purchases by corporations, associations, and others. For details, contact the "Special Sales Department" at the Berrett-Koehler address above.

Individual sales. Berrett-Koehler publications are available through most bookstores. They can also be ordered directly from Berrett-Koehler: Tel: (800) 929-2929; Fax: (802) 864-7626; www.bkconnection.com.

Orders for college textbook / course adoption use. Please contact Berrett-Koehler: Tel: (800) 929-2929; Fax: (802) 864-7626.

Distributed to the U.S. trade and internationally by Penguin Random House Publisher Services.

Berrett-Koehler and the BK logo are registered trademarks of Berrett-Koehler Publishers, Inc.

Printed in the United States of America

Berrett-Koehler books are printed on long-lasting acid-free paper. When it is available, we choose paper that has been manufactured by environmentally responsible processes. These may include using trees grown in sustainable forests, incorporating recycled paper, minimizing chlorine in bleaching, or recycling the energy produced at the paper mill.

Library of Congress Cataloging-in-Publication Data

Names: Horn, Sabrina, author.
Title: Make it, don't fake it : leading with authenticity for real business
    success / Sabrina Horn.
Description: 1st Edition. | Oakland : Berrett-Koehler Publishers, 2021. |
    Includes bibliographical references and index.
Identifiers: LCCN 2021005976 | ISBN 9781523091492 (paperback) | ISBN
    9781523091508 (adobe pdf) | ISBN 9781523091515 (epub)
Subjects: LCSH: New business enterprises--Management. | Women executives. |
    Branding (Marketing) | Leadership.
Classification: LCC HD62.5 .H6477 2021 | DDC 658.4/092--dc23
LC record available at https://lccn.loc.gov/2021005976

Hardcover ISBN: 978-1-5230-0060-9

First Edition

29 28 27 26 25 24 23 22 21   10 9 8 7 6 5 4 3 2 1

Book producer and designer: Seventeenth Street Studios
Cover designer: Susan Malikowski, DesignLeaf Studio
Author photo: David Katzive

CONTENTS

Foreword   vii

Introduction   1

Chapter One: Some Really Bad Advice   11

Chapter Two: So, You Want to Start a Company . . .   31

Chapter Three: Becoming a CEO   51

Chapter Four: Becoming and Staying an Authentic Brand   71

Chapter Five: Get Used to Lonely   97

Chapter Six: Airtight   113

Chapter Seven: *Leader* and *Loser* Both Begin
                    with the Letter *L*   131

Chapter Eight: Way Off the Menu   145

Chapter Nine: The Founder's Curse   165

Notes   180
Acknowledgments   184
Index   187
About the Author   192
About Horn Strategy, LLC   194

For Grace and Christina

FOREWORD

In 1991, Sabrina Horn and I both left well-established high-tech PR firms to hang out our own shingles, and we both had enough success to establish full-fledged consulting firms—The Horn Group and The Chasm Group, respectively. We also spent most of that decade interoperating and supporting each other during a major expansion of the high-tech sector, driven largely by the enterprises we were both targeting as customers. At the same time, Horn Group was instrumental in helping me launch a series of business books that drove business to our firm, while I was helpful to Sabrina in working through the strategy, positioning, and organizational challenges that come with scaling a fast-growing business. All this to say I am deeply familiar with the person, the events, and the challenges that are at the heart of the book you are about to read.

It is an important book for our times. Faking it is a loser's game. It may take a while to catch up with you, but when it does, the reckoning is brutal. Making it is a winner's game. It takes grit, it takes commitment, and yes, it takes some luck too, but most of all, win or lose, it is a game you can walk away from with your head held high. Life is not a dress rehearsal. There are no do-overs. It is important for us to be our best selves, to bring our best to our endeavors, to serve the ones we care about as best we can. This is especially true for anyone who wants to found a company.

Peter Drucker famously said, "The purpose of a business is to create a customer." How hard can that be? As you will see, it is not only hard, it is hard in different ways, depending on how big your company is, what opportunities are in play, and what headwinds or tailwinds are blowing at the time. Sabrina has been through the gamut, from start-up to exit into a large enterprise, from navigating the evolution of the PR industry to multiple cycles of the tech industry, and from counseling her clients into positions of market leadership, through crises, and finally to their own exits.

At every stage in this journey, there were good times and bad, but it is especially illuminating to learn how she faced up to the tough times, what they had to teach her, and what she had to be humble enough to learn from. If you are an entrepreneur, her journey is your journey, and you will have much to learn from it.

Entrepreneurship, through a series of highly visible success stories, has become a popular identity theme for a whole generation. Unfortunately, somewhere along the way, the idea crossed the line between reality and fantasy. It became a pose, where anyone with a half-baked idea fancied themselves achieving instant success, pockets filled with easy money. This is "faking it," pure and simple.

Fake it till you make it is a little more complicated. Entrepreneurs often do not know if they are making the right choices, and they do make commitments well before they have all the facts. But as Sabrina makes clear, that is not faking it, that is *risking it*. Faking it is when you shrink from risk and shirk responsibility from commitments if they don't work out. Entrepreneurs don't say, "It wasn't my fault"—not because they are nobler than the rest of us but because they want to learn from their mistakes, and the only way to do that is to take responsibility for them.

At the end of the day, this is a book about integrity, not as a pose or a positioning statement but as a platform for creating customers and delivering value to them. It is about the intellectual and emotional challenges of leadership. Sabrina is particularly good at communicating her personal experience with these challenges, dealing squarely with both the highs and the lows. Her insights are worth taking to heart, and her courage is worth emulating.

Geoffrey Moore
Author of *Crossing the Chasm* and *Zone to Win*

INTRODUCTION

"Making it" is at the heart of what drives every entrepreneur, executive, CEO, and founder. We strive to
achieve success. For sure, none of us decides to start or lead a
company with the intent to fail. Yet, in the course of running
our companies, we may sabotage potential success by taking
shortcuts, setting ourselves and our businesses back. Or worse,
falling prey to a lapse of confidence, a lack of information, or
a loss of stamina, we may stray from the trail we are blazing.
Either way, we think maybe it's easier to fake it, maybe just this
once or maybe some more.

Of all the business and career memes to gain popularity,
few have compromised integrity in business, leadership, and
personal success more than the expression "Fake it till you
make it." With roots in well-intentioned early twentieth-century
psychotherapy, this phrase has degenerated into a mantra that
has encouraged and even normalized lying for the purpose of
getting ahead. Now a product of modern American culture that
rolls all too easily off the tongue, its mere existence tells you
it's okay to lie, from twisting the truth just a little to flagrantly
deceiving others for personal gain.

Gender neutral, tempting both the young and the experienced, faking it has been baked into our society. This is unfortunately all too often apparent at the leadership level in business, where the fake it ethos can permeate entire corporations, putting millions of people and billions of dollars at risk.

Ponzi king Bernie Madoff and disgraced former Theranos CEO and tech queen Elizabeth Holmes are spectacular cases in point, but most fakery occurs in more routine and less egregious scenarios. Rising executives may feign their educational pedigree to snag a top job, entrepreneurs may exaggerate product capabilities to raise capital, salespeople overpromise to win their deals, and even seasoned CEOs sometimes look the other way when their backs are to the wall.

Let's face it, we've all probably faked it in some way, at some time, in the name of getting something we want to have or dodging something we want to avoid.

My mission in this book is to help people achieve business success with integrity by dismantling the fake it till you make it ethos, which only serves to corrupt integrity and hinder long-term success. While I wrote it for anyone who is or wants to be in a position of leadership, it will resonate most with entrepreneurs, founders, rising executives, and occupants of the C-suites of privately held companies. This group includes the ecosystem of investors, board members, advisors, and mentors who surround a business. It is also for the generation of career-ascending millennials and Gen Zers who have been so inculcated with the whole fake it mantra.

My motive and license are the unique double perspective I have as a founder and CEO of my own communications firm in the tech industry *and* as a strategic advisor to more than a thousand tech executives, venture capitalists, and influencers. I bring to the table twenty-five years of painful mistakes, gratifying successes, and useful lessons from running my company, as well as the insights from helping, typically from behind the curtain, so many other leaders through their own, often dicey "situations."

WHAT YOU CAN EXPECT

This is a book about ethics, passion, confidence, pride, resilience, commitment, and survival in a business context. It is about doing the right thing, which requires doing the right *things* the right *way*. This almost always means doing them the *hard* way. It is about becoming a leader, building a company culture and brand based on strong core values, managing both growth and decline, dealing with loneliness and with losing, facing a plethora of crises, and profitably selling your business.

It is about doing all this while staying grounded in reality, with integrity and some modicum of grace.

In this book, I present practical strategies, tools, ideas, and straight-up advice to protect you, as a leader, from faking it. I share how to recognize and avoid the damaging consequences of a range of opportunities to fake it that can arise in certain business situations. I offer frameworks and mental maps born out of decades of spinning a million plates to help you navigate complex business decisions and lead with greater confidence and resilience. Indeed, I have been careful not to confuse faking it with being efficient and pragmatic. Not every decision needs to turn into some deep internal moral debate.

This book is about achieving success—about "making it"—and knowing that you don't need to fake it at all. The truth is, real leadership and business success cannot be faked, not in the long run, anyway. Faking it is never sustainable. After a while—in a few minutes, weeks, or decades—the fraud falls apart. The employer will uncover the lies in the résumé, the investor will discover that the entrepreneur's technology doesn't perform as specified, the customer will find out that the salesperson's product doesn't deliver as promised. What was meant to be a triumph becomes a defeat.

A QUICK HISTORY

If faking it is so futile, why did it gain such popular acceptance?

The closest thing to a birth certificate for the fake it mantra/meme is a February 1, 1973, document from the US Court of Appeals for the Ninth Circuit denying an appeal of a Securities and Exchange Commission injunction against Glenn W. Turner Enterprises. The specific Turner company, called Dare to Be Great, was operating an illegal pyramid scheme in which prospects were persuaded to buy phony self-improvement classes called "Adventures." Once they became customers, these same people were instructed to sell to others the very same classes they had bought, thereby perpetuating the scheme. They were told to say that Dare to Be Great had made them rich. Of course, it had done no such thing, and they were instructed to lie—that is, to just "fake it till you make it."[1] The phrase is cited, word for word, in the appellate court's decision, probably being its first appearance in print.

There also are aspects of fake it till you make it—but not the phrase itself—rooted in psychology. During the 1920s, Austrian physician and psychotherapist Alfred Adler introduced a technique he called "acting as if" to speed up the process of psychotherapy. Adler encouraged patients to simply practice alternatives to their dysfunctional behaviors, telling them to "act as if" they were the person they wanted to be by imagining and then practicing those behaviors. His insights have been incorporated into modern cognitive behavioral therapy, which uses a similar approach and helps people suffering from depression and anxiety.

Science supports faking it till you make it, but only to a point. For Adler, "acting as if" was not proposed as a cure for mental illness. It was just a sort of therapeutic kick-start *toward* a cure. The same is true of today's cognitive behavioral therapy. Finding alternatives to dysfunctional behavior and practicing them are steps *toward* changing thoughts and feelings. They are a means, not an end.

You don't have to look far to find current pop psychology versions of Adler's "as if." Take Amy Cuddy, a former Harvard social psychologist who became a minor pop culture sensation with a 2012 TED talk that promoted her theory (developed with fellow psychologist Dana R. Carney) of "power posing."[2] The idea is that if you assume a body posture you associate with being powerful, you quite literally position yourself to think, feel, and behave in more assertive ways. As she said in her talk, "Fake it till you *become* it." In 2016, Carney abandoned the theory, although Cuddy (as of this writing) continues to assert that "posture feedback" can at least make people feel more powerful.[3]

To give Cuddy her due, she is by no means suggesting that we fake it at someone else's expense, as in perpetrating a fraud. Her aim is to use posture as a way to heighten personal feelings of self-confidence. While the theory may be questionable, the motive is blameless. After all, building self-confidence is both therapeutic and liberating.

Yet the phrase "Fake it till you make it" has become irretrievably tainted, having been mindlessly propagated and supercharged through social media and then further mutated with overuse. In 2008, *Faking It: How to Seem Like a Better Person Without Actually Improving Yourself* was published as a parody by authors billed as "the writers of CollegeHumor.com." There was even a TV series in 2010 called *Fake It Til You Make It*, which made it through eight episodes of people faking each other out before it was canceled.

As a meme, the concept has crossed the bright red line. "Acting as if" to innocently build one's confidence has turned into faking it by exaggerating, minimizing, or otherwise fabricating the truth at the expense of others. It is so commonplace, in both our personal and our professional lives, that we've become numb to it. It has become acceptable advice as a means to make it—to achieve success—and most unfortunately, as a really bad excuse for bad leadership.

WHY SHOULD YOU LISTEN TO ME?

I wrote this book from a unique dual perspective, as a woman who learned how to be a leader of her own company *and* as someone who has helped thousands of other leaders manage through the good, the bad, and the sticky. For a quarter century, I was the founder and CEO of Horn Group, a public relations and marketing communications agency in the tech industry.

Whoa. I can see those eyebrows rising. *Isn't PR all about the art of spin? And if spin isn't fakery, it certainly is a second cousin.*

I get it. You may think that the idea of a PR person dispensing advice on integrity seems, to put it politely, unconventional, unexpected, and more frankly, unreal. But the truth is that being a PR pro means being a crusader *against* faking it. It has put me here to tell you that the only way to make it is not to fake it at all.

Done right, public relations has nothing to do with spin, a proverbial four-letter word in the biz. Indeed, there is a big difference in intent between misleading people by making something look better than it really is and simply bringing to life what is most compelling about it for the purpose of earning attention, interest, and trust. The best PR works to get to the truth, sets and resets expectations based on the truth, and communicates vital truths at the right time, in the right way, and to the right audiences. It helps CEOs and their companies behave and communicate more responsibly. The best PR *people* make themselves indispensable by becoming business experts who have communications expertise.

As my mentor Dr. Otto Lerbinger, professor emeritus of public relations at Boston University, taught in his classes, "Public relations seeks to understand what all the stakeholders of an organization want, need, and believe. In turn, it informs corporate leadership on how to move forward, guiding strategic change or prompting further diligence. PR professionals should strive to be evangelists for understanding reality, finding the truth, and practicing ethical leadership."

It is fair to say that this quest is also my personal mission, and one which I try to achieve through expert communications. Great communications makes relationships work, simplifies the complex, clarifies the obtuse, and stands for what is right. We certainly have all experienced what happens when there is a failure to communicate.

Being a communications professional and the CEO of a PR company was a heady responsibility, and one I took quite seriously. Our clients depended on us to help shape and tell their stories about technologies that had the power to change how people live and work. The media, with whom we forged confident, trusting relationships, relied on us for viable ideas and accurate information about our clients. The power of a single word often was the difference between creating clarity and adding to confusion—a lesson I have relearned in the writing of this book.

As a PR pro, I saw a lot. My company helped tech CEOs navigate the perils of board-level fraud and shady executive behavior, acquisitions canceled at the eleventh hour, security breaches, and products that failed in mission-critical environments. We kept *them* from faking it by getting to the truth and by facing the harsh realities that had to be confronted to find a path forward. Sometimes we turned prospective clients away or rejected what they proposed because what they stood for or what they wanted us to do was untrue, unethical, unrealistic, or simply crazy. *We* did not want to be complicit in *their* fakery.

My firm also facilitated much positive transformation in the tech industry, bringing breakthrough technologies to market, creating new product categories, and shaping the industry. We were change agents. We made technology understandable, acceptable, and even embraceable.

As a CEO of my own company, I managed through periods of warp-speed growth and devastating market contraction. I learned on the job how to become a leader by navigating almost every business scenario you can imagine, from building my team and evolving our service offering, to expanding geographically, to managing layoffs, to surviving the 2008–2009 recession and employee embezzlement, to rebuilding after 2012's devastating Hurricane Sandy, to leading the successful acquisition of my firm. There were delicate employee situations and stupid mistakes that cost us business. And then there was just the normal everyday work of running a firm and tending to clients. The level of commitment was deep and the consumption of energy enormous—definitely not something you can fake.

I did all this while raising my two daughters, Grace and Christina, on two coasts, mostly as a single parent.

KEEPING IT REAL

Through this time, I had the pleasure of employing a thousand people and the privilege of working with hundreds and hundreds of technology companies, from the hottest start-ups to the Fortune 500. With my leadership teams, I led Horn Group from being a single-office start-up to becoming a firm with multiple offices and global reach. We built an enduring, iconic brand in our sector, winning awards for our client work and accolades as a best employer and best tech agency in the United States. My company was privately held, an S corporation with no outside investors and with key employees who held equity that they could monetize when I finally sold it to Finn Partners, a global marketing communications firm, in 2015.

Yes, there were plenty of times I faked it. As you will see, every one of those times set me and my business back. I started my company with an idea and a whole lot of passion but no management skills, no customers, no employees, no money, and a four-page business plan. I made many mistakes and enjoyed my fair share of triumphs—learning, either way, from each decision, action, and result. These experiences are my research, and they are the inspiration and fodder for this book (some names and situations have been altered or modified for privacy). But my point here is this: whether you are a leader in a hundred-person service business, a $100 million company, or a Fortune 100 company, the problems and opportunities you face demand that you always act from a place of truth, reality, and integrity.

I wrote this book to help a generation of leaders make it. I wrote it to help these leaders, whether arriving or arrived, achieve long-term business success precisely because they *didn't* fake it.

Make It, Don't Fake It is intended to help you be more successful by making the right decisions at the right time, based on reality. Acting from a basis of truth, you will feel empowered to make effective decisions for the good of the many, not the one. Such is leading with authenticity for real business success.

CHAPTER ONE

SOME REALLY BAD ADVICE

As this is a book about achieving business success with integrity, it is important to understand something about why people lie. It is obvious that lying should not be our modus operandi, yet it happens all the time, in various forms and for different reasons. Understanding what compels people to fabricate the truth, to fake it, and to just plain lie is useful in coming up with the strategies and tools to avoid or prevent it.

There is a broad spectrum of fakery, from the perfectly innocent—Adler's "acting as if"—to the perfectly criminal. In what follows, I explain that continuum with examples. To help you visualize it, I offer my Fake-O-Meter (figure 1). Note that the phrase "FAKING IT" marks the point at which certain types of lies pass from relatively harmless to costing you and others time, money, and reputation.

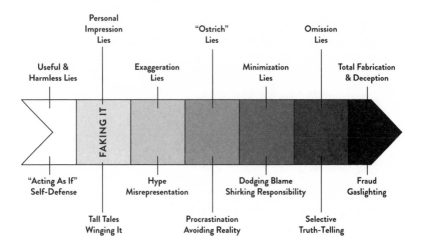

Personal
Impression
Lies

"Ostrich"
Lies

Omission
Lies

Useful &
Harmless Lies

Exaggeration
Lies

Minimization
Lies

Total Fabrication
& Deception

FAKING IT

"Acting As If"
Self-Defense

Hype
Misrepresentation

Dodging Blame
Shirking Responsibility

Fraud
Gaslighting

Tall Tales
Winging It

Procrastination
Avoiding Reality

Selective
Truth-Telling

FIGURE 1   Fake-O-Meter

THERAPEUTIC, USEFUL, AND NECESSARY LIES

Biologically, intellectually, politically, and morally, we live in an impure world. We have to make peace with that reality and navigate it as well as we can. But let's agree from the get-go that not all lies are equally bad and that some are therapeutic, useful, or even necessary. With this in mind, we can go on to define the degree of moral impurity with which we are willing to live.

Acting As If

As we saw in the introduction, Alfred Adler's confidence-building approach of "acting as if" is a therapeutic use of pretending (in this case a benign type of lying), with origins in psychology. You pretend—to yourself—to be more confident by acting as if you were as confident as you would like to be. The result, Adler and others have found, is that you actually *feel* more confident and, feeling confident, you perform as if you were truly confident. This may lead to more successful outcomes in your interactions, which serve to further reinforce your feelings of confidence. With a bit of luck, a virtuous circle is formed, in which successful outcomes produce greater confidence, which produce more successful outcomes, and so on.

"Acting as if" can be especially useful to anyone who suffers from imposter syndrome, the strong and even debilitating feeling that you are undeserving of your achievements. Those afflicted feel that they are frauds and fear that they will be exposed for faking their way to success, when in reality they never faked it at all and earned success honestly. People who already struggle with issues of self-efficacy and perfectionism often fall victim to "imposterism." It is actually a common disorder, affecting as many as a third of high achievers, both men and women. About 70% of adults experience it at least occasionally.[1]

If you are troubled by imposterism, "acting as if"— pretending how it would be if you felt that you were competent, accomplished, and deserving of praise and admiration—may help change how you feel. You can also reflect upon, assess, and appreciate your actual achievements. Inventory them, admire them, but do not compare them to the achievements of anyone else. Measure your own achievements, not those of others.

Other strategies in the "acting as if" category include "dressing for success"—for instance, wearing black or red to feel more powerful. Visualization also can be helpful when preparing to face new or potentially challenging situations, a practice I have often found helpful. I previsit the scene in my imagination as a way of rehearsing how it might unfold, thereby becoming more comfortable with how to navigate it. I call this watching myself in my own movie. The ethical common denominator in all of these forms of "acting as if" is that the pretending is strictly between you and your own imagination. No part of it is being done at the expense of another person.

But can "acting as if" cross the line from therapy to actually faking it? And can that faking be undertaken to the detriment of someone else? Absolutely.

While you cross no ethical line by faking confidence itself, you must not fake external reasons to back up your confidence. For example, you may act as if you are confident that your business proposal is a winner, but if you tell a prospect that you have the data to prove it when no such data exists, you are crossing an ethical line, and quite possibly a legal one as well.

The Little White Lie

"Little white lie" is one of those expressions that everyone believes they understand but which turns out to have a wide and remarkably vague range of meaning. Some believe a white lie is any benign, trivial, or harmless falsehood. The problem with this definition is that it leaves far too much to individual judgment; what I might consider trivial and harmless, someone else may find scandalous. Besides that, even telling trivial lies may get you busted and, therefore, branded as a liar or a fibber. Either way, people may become reluctant to trust you.

The safer definition is to think of a white lie as something you say to be polite, to avoid hurting someone's feelings, or to avoid upsetting someone unnecessarily.

WIFE: "Does this outfit make me look fat?"

HUSBAND: "You look gorgeous in anything."

Often, a white lie takes the form of rendering an opinion that is absolutely the most positive you can come up with. At a dinner party, your host serves a spectacularly bland meal.

HOST: "How did you like the fish?"

YOU: "I loved the delicate flavor."

In a business context, white lies are often a disservice. Whenever a client asked me for my opinion, I told the truth, though I sometimes modulated it to be as constructive as possible within the confines of the truth. For instance, if something the client proposed was flawed, I would try to comment truthfully on what was good about it and use that positive element as a platform from which to suggest improvements. With respect to my own feelings, this was a white lie. For the purposes of making a suboptimal project better, however, it avoided demoralizing or even alienating the client while moving the project toward improvement.

Finally, white lies can reduce life's friction from day to day.

"How are you?" is among the most conventional greetings we offer one another. Sometimes, however, you have a headache, feel anxious, or didn't get a good night's sleep. But do you really want to get into all that? So you answer, "Just fine. And you?"

Necessary Lies

The third type of "innocent" lying in this category is necessary lies. The sudden, unexpected loss of a loved one may be met with denial or a refusal to acknowledge reality. Such evasion of facts is not immoral or unethical. Indeed, it may be an emotionally necessary or at least unavoidable initial response to the loss.

Or consider this: an EMT arriving on an accident scene begins treating a gravely injured man.

"Am I going to die?" the victim gasps.

Acting on a strictly professional assessment, the most accurate answer might well be "Yes, probably." But the medic knows the value of hope and responds instead, "No. Hang in there. We are going to take very good care of you!"

And finally, people lie to protect their privacy and that of their family. They may lie in situations of physical danger, to save themselves or others. These are necessary lies and there is no argument there.

FAKING IT: THE BRIGHT RED LINE

It is at this point that "acting as if" and other types of lies in this category cross a threshold into faking it, because the fakery is being conducted at another person's expense, albeit without malice. Anxious to make a good impression or to avoid making a bad one, we may tell a tall tale, twist, cover up, augment, wing it, deliberately deform, or evade the truth. A personal lack of confidence, insecurity, or a perceived inadequacy leads many of us into this kind of fakery. These types of lies are more interpersonal, simpler, and not as egregious as others we discuss later, as measured on the Fake-O-Meter.

Twisting and Evading

It was the summer before my senior year in high school and I had a job working at a popular stationery store in town. The owners, a nice elderly couple from Poland, sold magazines, chewing gum, cigars, cigarettes, baseball cards, candy, stuff like that. I often thought that maybe someday I could own a nice little store like this, too.

The thing is, they ran an open cash register business; they never shut the cash drawer to ring up a sale. It was just money in and change out. With every sale, I had to do the math in my head, even calculating the sales tax. Unfortunately, I just couldn't add or subtract that quickly, and I was too embarrassed to ask for a pencil and paper. Using the cash register was out of the question; it would have required them to change their business model. I wanted the owners to think I was smart, like them.

It went down like this. A customer would walk up to the counter with a magazine, some gum, a pack of cigarettes, and a couple of greeting cards. I'd act like I was doing the mental arithmetic and then arrived at some random number that might be acceptable.

"Uh, sure. That'll be eight dollars, please," I'd say, hoping the customer's reaction would be positive.

Maybe the figure was close. Maybe it wasn't. In reality, it was total improv. One hundred percent.

Amazingly, it worked—for a little while. But the day of reckoning came, when the owners realized I was essentially giving their merchandise away. With admirable patience, they presented me with the pad of paper and pencil I should have asked for in the first place. It certainly was easier, writing it all down, but they stood over me and watched me like a pair of hawks. The surveillance was so unnerving, I still couldn't add or subtract on the fly, especially when someone gave me a twenty to break on a $3.28 sale.

I did not make it at the stationery store. I was fired, and I learned my first hard lesson in the consequences of faking it. In retrospect, that lesson may not have been hard enough. Certainly, I had no intention of cheating my employers, but cheat them I certainly did. This instance of fake it till you make it was at their expense, and thus I had blithely crossed the line into petty fraud.

Tall Tales

In my twenties, I learned the fake it lesson again. This time, though, I did it for love. I wanted to impress Jeff, an entrepreneur who had his own start-up, and when the subject turned to skiing, I mentioned that I loved downhill.

"Really?" he asked.

"More than anything."

"You any good?"

"I'm double black diamond good," I laughed.

At this, he invited me to ski the double black diamond run at Squaw Valley, the site of the 1960 Winter Olympics, near Lake Tahoe, California. I figured, how hard could it be? Growing up on the East Coast, I had skied on sheer ice in Vermont and New Hampshire and was a decent intermediate skier.

Without skipping a beat, I accepted, and he made the arrangements.

When I got off the chairlift at the top of the mountain, I thought I was going to die. This was it; game over. Call the chopper, bring the stretcher. Eventually pulling myself together, I slid down the entire vertical drop on my side. Clearly, faking it had not worked for me. I definitely wasn't going to make it with Jeff, either.

Winging It

Fast-forward a few years to when, as a young executive, I was sitting in front of a client who was going on and on about some new technology he wanted us to promote. Wanting to impress him, I nodded my head in bogus understanding, though I didn't have a clue what he was talking about.

Did I pull it off? Yeah. Did I have to backtrack? Usually.

I never felt great about it, and it was kind of stressful. I should have just brought the discussion back to how we could help him from a marketing standpoint, or suggested that we do a deep dive into his technology at some other time. In the moment, I didn't have the confidence to stop, ask a question, or redirect the conversation. It would have been *so* simple. But then, hindsight is the Great Simplifier.

There also were side effects I had to consider. As a leader, you are always under a microscope. If I faked it, others around me would likely follow my example. Even small acts of fakery, harmless in themselves, nurture a let's-just-wing-it culture, which I did not want to create in my company. Sometimes in business, you *do* just have to wing it. That is also a reality. Yet it is the proverbial exception that proves the rule. Winging it, more often than not, is faking it and therefore is not a sustainable business practice.

EXAGGERATION LIES

Exaggeration is the false assertion that something is greater or better than it actually is. It is one of the most common ways to fake it till you make it in business today. Instances of exaggeration, their eventual exposure, and the resulting consequences range widely in severity.

A really popular example is lying on your résumé or in a job interview to appear more accomplished. In fact, a 2017 study revealed that 85% of employers caught applicants lying on résumés or applications.[2] Other common examples of lying through exaggeration include inflating a product's actual capabilities to garner more customers or to secure venture capital (VC) funding, and overstating company revenues to attain a higher valuation. At any point, the fakery can be exposed. The customers or VCs will discover that the product doesn't do what management promised and the auditors will uncover the faulty financials. The consequences can range from losing professional credibility or a job opportunity, to losing financial support, customers, and revenue, to getting sued and, at a still-realistic extreme, facing criminal prosecution. Definitely not the right strategy to achieve success.

Hype Cycle Lies

Hype is a kind of exaggerational fakery prevalent within marketing and PR, which are all about image and perception building. It is more sophisticated and broader in scope than simply twisting the truth a little to impress a friend. I cannot begin to tell you how many times prospective clients came to us saying, "Build our buzz. Make us a hot company to watch!" If I had a nickel, as they say.

Thankfully, there are ways of building brands for companies that actually deserve to be "hot," as you'll see in chapter 4. The harder trick, I discovered, was helping those companies that were viable but perhaps less interesting "wannabes," while also steering clear of the ones that thought they could use PR to be something they could never live up to. The bottom line, as I mentioned in the introduction, was always an exercise in identifying their "real" story, remaining within the boundaries of the truth while also highlighting what was genuinely most interesting, beneficial, or different. As our clients' agents or representatives, this was as much an exercise in advising them on what not to say ("We're going to close a huge deal next week that's going to be a real game changer!") as it was in communi-cating their true stories ("The benefits our current customers are experiencing are an indicator of early market traction.").

Company credibility and reputation are all based on track record, on what you have achieved. They also are based on what you are accomplishing, how you conduct yourself, what you stand for and from which you never veer. That's making it. And the only way we could make it for them—and ourselves, for that matter—was to not fake it.

Build It and They Will Come!

Now imagine that not one but all of your customers and com-petitors are in an industry bubble, an economic cycle marked by the rapid escalation and exaggeration of market value. As former US Federal Reserve chairman Alan Greenspan put it during the 1998–2000 Internet boom, it was the era of "irrational exuberance."

During this period, VCs funded almost any start-up boasting an online platform. Business software companies catapulted to success by creating the infrastructure for this e-commerce. New market categories were created literally overnight. Companies were swept up into the tornado of success, quickly went public or got acquired, and generated lucrative returns, many of them only on paper. It was a modern-day gold rush.

"Build it and they will come," a phrase made popular by Kevin Costner's 1989 movie *Field of Dreams*, was the mantra of the time. And everyone in the tech ecosystem wanted to be in that movie: lawyers, bankers, publicists, consultants, analysts, the media itself. My company was caught up in it, too. There weren't enough tech PR people on the planet to support all the business we could have taken on. Prospects offered us free stock and three months' retainer if we "saved them a slot" on our roster. Feeding into the frenzy, we decided to open a branch office in Seattle in late 2000.

That office did not last long. We built it. They did not come. End of story.

A famous example of the dot-com era is Pets.com, one of the first companies to sell pet supplies online. The company spent a great deal of money marketing a cute canine sock puppet as its public face, and it even managed to get the puppet interviewed by *People* magazine and *Good Morning America*. The company's executives never really thought through the whole business model behind the sock puppet, however, and on November 9, 2000, it put itself to sleep. Rivals like Petopia.com, which recruited some of my employees with stock options and huge salaries, soon folded, too, along with hundreds of other companies.

The great majority of the tech execs of this era were not deliberately or criminally deceitful. Some had great ideas but no business being CEOs. Others had great leadership experience but went into the public markets too early, with no profits, incredibly high valuations, and unproven business models. Still others had technology that wasn't quite ready for prime time. It was a type of fakery in which substance was overlooked and blind ambition and, yes, hype and greed took over.

Pets.com and countless first-generation Web start-ups never figured out how to build real businesses. They were based on a variant of fake it till you make it called build it and they will come. They made it—for a short time—but with a flawed strategy, and they all eventually ran out of time and money.

Hot Seat Lies

Let's look at the time when we were recovering from the Great Recession of 2008 to 2009 and my company really needed to ramp up revenue. On a sales and business development rampage, I put myself out there and led a pitch to win a half-million-dollar account, a comprehensive integrated marketing campaign for a company in the financial technology software space. This would be a huge piece of business, and winning it would really help our situation.

Did we have the skills in-house to do the work I promised? *I would find them!*

Did we have the bandwidth to lead such a complicated campaign?

I'll put my best people on it!

Can we get them a story in *The Wall Street Journal*?

Whatever. Sure.

Exasperated and under serious pressure, we punched above our weight and faked our capabilities. Having exaggerated our capacity, we were behind the eight ball before we even started. Our recommendations were off the mark and the cofounders did not care for our delays and excuses. We made the head of marketing who hired us look bad. Bit by bit, we lost pieces of that account—until we lost it all, along with a chunk of our credibility. It sucked. I learned the lesson, and it cost me and my organization.

Overconfident and Arrogant Lies

During my career, I've met a lot of tech executives who were, shall we say, "overly optimistic" about the viability of their businesses. They were all trying to make it, strutting their stuff with greatly exaggerated stories of what their products could do, in the hope that we, in turn, would project that image to the press. To convey the *real* facts about our clients, we required that every engagement begin with an assessment of actual versus future capabilities, current installed base, and customer endorsements. We asked to see their business plans, spoke with their investors, and in some cases, even reviewed their financials. We did our best to not get caught up in their fakery.

"We are leaders in the supply chain software market and have customers around the world," one start-up founder arrogantly told me.

I don't think so, Mr. Founder, I said to myself. *You have five other competitors, all much larger than you, zero revenues to date, and exactly three customers—to whom you gave your product for free. Also, nobody cares.*

I almost took pleasure in dismantling his claims.

Once, I even met a man at a software conference who introduced himself as the CEO of a start-up and said he wanted to retain our firm to handle his PR. Terrific! Except it turned out that he was not the CEO—which was just as well, because there was no start-up, either.

There are countless stories like these, some ridiculous, others sobering, and many just pathetic. Looking back, most of the infractions were relatively innocuous. Lessons were learned, mistakes corrected, apologies offered, and people moved on.

OSTRICH LIES

In this category, the person involved may be either intentionally or unintentionally kicking problems under the rug, unduly procrastinating, or, like the stereotyped ostrich, sticking their head in the sand, all because they are so utterly overwhelmed with the situation at hand and what lies ahead.[3] Sometimes the truth is that, as an entrepreneur or business leader, you simply *don't* know what to do. You hope it will all go away, and you want to pretend everything is fine. This is faking it, because at the moment, you are not dealing squarely with reality.

Unfortunately, the evasion comes at everyone else's expense. It's extremely dangerous, because you're at risk of waiting too long to formulate a plan of action, putting all your stakeholders and the viability of your business in jeopardy, and dragging everyone down with you.

As a young female executive running a tech PR firm, I came head to head with this.

In 2001, already in business for ten years, we had some of the top software companies in the industry as clients, a strong brand, and a good reputation. But as the Internet bubble was bursting all around us, our clients were cutting their budgets almost daily. The business I had worked so hard to build was evaporating. Being eight months pregnant with my second daughter, Christina, I had other thoughts on my mind. I wanted to pretend everything was okay and that it would all just get better.

"Hope is not a strategy, Sabrina," one of my advisors told me. "You have to protect the financial health of your company and let some people go."

It became abundantly clear that if I wanted to have any chance at continued success, at making it, let alone at surviving the tech bust, I would have to face reality. I had never done a layoff before, but I did it then, and it nearly destroyed me. Having to let people go whom *I* had hired filled me with guilt. Professionally, the layoff was a tremendous setback for the business, a loss of forward momentum, of revenue, and of the ability to serve our clients. Personally, it came at a time when I was trying to focus on having my baby. The layoff pulled me away from mindfulness of that incredible life experience.

This was one of many hard lessons I learned about real leadership. Running a successful business means making the right decisions at the right time, based on reality. It also means making those decisions for the greater good of the *whole* company, often in the face of great disruption and painful change. Eliminating jobs was awful, but using up all our cash reserves, potentially going bankrupt and losing everything, would have been much worse. I had to choose the lesser of two evils. I chose the former, which would prevent the latter from happening. It was the right strategic move.

MINIMIZATION LIES: SHIRKING RESPONSIBILITY AND DODGING BLAME

The opposite of the exaggeration lie is the minimization lie, which seeks to lessen the extent and consequences of a bad situation by shirking responsibility and dodging blame. Minimization lies often involve rationalization and take place when people can't completely deny the truth.[4] A well-known example is from the mid-1980s, when vacuum cleaner maker Regina changed management and brought out products that were less expensive to manufacture. The problem was that the cheaper plastic parts sometimes melted, and customer returns rose to some 16% of gross sales revenues. The new CEO cooked the books to understate the losses in advance of an audit. Eventually, the defects outpaced management's ability to hide the losses, and the company collapsed with a loss to investors and creditors of some $40 million.[5]

OMISSION LIES: SELECTIVE TRUTH TELLING

Lying by omission is as common as telling white lies or fibbing, but, depending on the nature and scope of the omission, it can be grossly deceptive. Here, you are actually telling the truth, but you also are leaving out certain critically important facts, creating misconception in an effort to move something forward. For many people, omission is easier than other types of lying because it doesn't involve making anything up and is therefore more passive.

For example, you might say, "I went to the meeting and we had a productive discussion," while omitting the fact that part of the discussion centered on radical budget cuts. Or you might mention that you parked the car in the garage and turned off the lights, but leave out the part where you arrived home at three a.m., hit the back wall, and smashed the headlight.

In the corporate world, lies of omission can be grave indeed. Take the example of Boeing's 737 Max aircraft, which suffered from technical problems that resulted in two deadly crashes, in 2018 and 2019, and killed 346 people. The tragedies were investigated by the US House of Representatives Committee on Transportation and Infrastructure, which found a "lack of transparency"—in short, lying by omission—to be a major factor in the failure to correct defects that directly resulted in the accidents.[6]

OUTRIGHT DECEPTION: THE HIGH COST OF FAKING IT

On the continuum of faking it, there are, of course, extremes. People who shamelessly lie to manipulate other people do so on purpose to mislead and deceive for personal gain. They fail to consider others' well-being or safety, and they intentionally lie at others' expense, to put themselves in a better position.

Manipulative lying includes *gaslighting*, a form of psychological deception in which a person covertly sows seeds of doubt in a targeted individual or group, making them question their own memory, perception, or judgment. To this person, buying or even stealing success might seem more rewarding than putting in the work to earn it.

Fabrication lies are entirely untrue and made-up stories. These lies can be at least in part delusional, but most are intentional, and they often are the product of desperation.

People who lie in such deliberately deceptive ways end up depending on the people to whom they have lied in order to perpetuate the fiction. In so doing, they lose their independence and sink deeper into an ongoing pattern of compulsive lying. Take Bernie Madoff and his massive Ponzi scheme, a fraud worth nearly $65 billion. He faked it till he made it and then ventured far beyond that, into the largest financial fraud in US history. Madoff ruined thousands of lives and ultimately received a term of 150 years in federal prison. The night before his arrest, Madoff finally told the truth, announcing to his family, "It's all just one big lie."[7]

Why did he do it? In 2011, Madoff answered this question for Harvard Business School professor Eugene Soltes, who interviewed him for a study on white-collar crime: "In hindsight, when I look back, it wasn't as if I couldn't have said no. . . . It wasn't like I was being blackmailed into doing something, or that I was afraid of getting caught doing it. . . . I sort of rationalized that what I was doing was OK, that it wasn't going to hurt anybody." Madoff added, "There was nothing that . . . I couldn't attain. . . . I was able to convince myself that this was, you know, a temporary situation."[8]

Madoff's statement goes a long way toward explaining the fake it till you make it trap. The faker succeeds in convincing himself that his fraud is temporary, a kind of stopgap measure on the way to making it. Yet, somehow, the "making it" never arrives, and the "temporary" fraud becomes permanent. No longer a tactic, the fakery becomes a strategy—and then a business model. By embracing this, Madoff inflicted around $64.8 billion in losses on his clients.[9]

A second, more recent example of a big-time faker is Elizabeth Holmes, the former CEO of Theranos. After dropping out of Stanford, she started Theranos to "democratize health care" with a fully automated digital device capable of testing a variety of diseases using just a pinprick of blood. Despite the small army of experts who told her that what she proposed was virtually impossible, she was still able to persuade venture capitalists to fork over $500 million in funding. She won a lucrative and highly publicized partnership with Walgreens, as well as with other health care organizations, and was running a company valued at $9 billion in 2014.

But Holmes ran her company in secrecy and did not unveil its mysterious yet much-hyped Edison prototype device until 2015. A few insiders began leaking stories of how Edison produced wildly inaccurate blood analysis results. Reporter John Carreyrou of *The Wall Street Journal* investigated the leaks and published a blockbuster story that essentially blew up the company, exposing the Edison device as, quite simply, massively failed technology.[10] In 2018, Holmes settled a Securities and Exchange Commission lawsuit for fraud, surrendered control of her company, and paid a half-million-dollar fine.

Why did Holmes do it? Whether she is in denial or delusional or both, she has never admitted wrongdoing and, in a

2017 deposition, said the words "I don't know" six hundred times.[11] According to Jessie Deeter, a producer of an HBO documentary on Holmes and Theranos, those who know Holmes best claim that "she really believed her own story. . . . She believed her own bullshit."[12] Yet she clearly faked it, made it, got caught, and lost it all. As of this writing, she is under indictment and, amid speculation about a possible insanity defense, faces up to twenty years' imprisonment if convicted.

SIMPLY BAD ADVICE

Yes, there are big differences, both in magnitude and in motivation, between my faux math in my hometown stationery store, my skiing disaster, and my missteps as an inexperienced CEO; the irrational exuberance of tech CEOs in the late nineties; and Madoff's and Holmes's multiyear reigns of fraud. The degree of deception and self-deception runs from a laughable infraction to the most unthinkable of crimes. In the extreme cases, the *faking it* rolls on and on, even as the *making it* recedes deeper into a future that never arrives. Faking it becomes a way of doing business and a way of living life—at least until the truth comes out and the game ends.

Bottom line: People fake it to attain *something* for themselves, whether that is for good reasons or bad. In all cases (except for self-help, self-defense, or politeness), whether a short-term tactic or a permanent strategy, it is at someone else's expense and it is never the "right" thing to do. It is never a recipe for long-term business success. It certainly is not what real leaders practice. It is simply bad advice.

REAL LEADERSHIP FOR THE REST OF US

True leaders search for what they can give; others search for what they can take. Most CEOs and business leaders locate their leadership style somewhere between these two poles. Some drift back and forth between them, often unpredictably. Still others aspire to truth in leadership but settle for a lot less. Some— *some*—prove to be real leaders, the kind who build their brands and lead enterprises that stand the test of time and are based on core principles of honesty, integrity, and a healthy dose of humility. That doesn't mean they don't make mistakes; they just make them honestly.

This book was not written for the Madoffs or Holmeses of the world. They are beyond hope. This book is for the rest of us, the entrepreneurs, business leaders, and CEOs who need to be pragmatic and are working toward a realistic promise of success. We want to grow our businesses the right way. We are well-intentioned and want to be good leaders. We face challenges every day. Some challenges are temptations to fake it, to shove a problem under the rug, or to minimize what is going on. Most are opportunities to be 100% authentic, while others demand a compromise between the fake and the real.

There is no textbook for how to deal with these situations, and there is no road map for success. It is all about the "getting there," the *journey* to making it, which is what matters most in authentic leadership.

Are you equipped to face reality in a career-creating, life-defining opportunity to make your own destiny? For me, both the question and the answer took place in the fires of Dresden, Germany, many years before I was born.

CHAPTER TWO

SO, YOU WANT TO START A COMPANY...

Dresden, Germany. The night of February 13, 1945. Nearly four thousand tons of high-explosive and incendiary bombs are being dropped by a combined Allied armada of 1,249 heavy bombers. Reduced to 1,600 acres of kindling, the city's buildings feed a massive firestorm in which Fahrenheit temperatures reach an incredible 2,700 degrees. In the small suburb of Mockritz, five miles away, three teenage women use a shovel to manhandle an unexploded firebomb that has landed on the roof of their home. Together, they manage to coax it off the roof and down onto a septic area, where it detonates, moving one entire side of the house out by a foot. The oldest of the three would become my mother; the younger two, my aunts.

From Dresden, Germany, to Charleston, West Virginia, to New York and then San Francisco, my parents survived and then, in postwar America, thrived. But it was the fact of their survival that drove their success. My mother had pushed a bomb off a roof. The man she loved, my father to be, was a paratrooper in the Resistance. He came to the United States in 1957 with $60 in his pockets and found success as a chemist, inventor, serial entrepreneur and CEO, Fortune 100 company executive, and venture capitalist. Throughout my childhood, I would hear their words: "Sabrina, you *have* to control your own destiny. You must *never* give up. There is no free lunch in life."

My parents never believed in luck. For one thing, they were scientists. Luck is unreliable. You better make your own "luck," they told me. With sharpened survival instincts, they anticipated every risk that came their way and crafted tactics to manage every hazard. They survived *and* thrived, and their example inspired me and continues to drive me to this day. I believe that this notion of controlling one's own destiny and having a keen survival instinct are in the heart of every company founder and CEO, and at the heart of leadership and the entrepreneurial spirit.

Of course, what drives you will be different from what drives me. That doesn't matter. What does matter is that you find your inspiration, fire, and inner conviction. And whatever *it* is, it had better be a passion powerful and personally meaningful enough to keep you on your path and to see you through the darkest, most unimaginable situations possible.

There was only one way to control my own destiny, and that was to become an entrepreneur—the driver and innovator of *something* that would serve a market, solve a problem, and make a positive difference.

CONTROL YOUR OWN DESTINY

Walnut Creek, California, 1991—about sixteen miles east of Oakland and no different from other Bay Area towns then sprouting the companies of Silicon Valley. Having taken a vacation day from work, and under a clear blue sky, I pulled into the parking lot of PeopleSoft, a business software company founded just four years earlier. There was a buzz about that company. It had an experienced leadership team led by successful tech executive David Duffield, and it was backed by Norwest Venture Partners, a venture capital firm affiliated with a finance company from Minneapolis. But, with maybe fifty employees and a handful of corporate customers, it was still definitely a start-up.

And yet a start-up was a lot more than I had at the time. In my car were all my tangible corporate assets: eighty 8½ x 11 transparencies to be shown on an overhead projector, which even in Silicon Valley was the state of technology for in-person presentations in 1991.

I walked into PeopleSoft's main conference room armed with a pack of business cards emblazoned with the initial name of my future company, Sabrina Horn Public Relations, and a logo that resembled a towel monogram. I had no employees, no clients, and except for the business cards, no evidence of a company, really. It was pretty ballsy. At twenty-nine years old, I did have about four years' job experience doing PR in the business-to-business (B2B) software tech space and a graduate degree in public relations, for which I had written a thesis on marketing high technology.

I also had a Big Idea in my head, based on a very short business plan I wrote while on vacation. It would continue to evolve over time, but it became the blueprint for my business and the first declaration of my company's values and culture. In it, I explained my vision for the kind of tech companies I wanted to go after and the PR services I would offer. I developed a landscape—a kind of ecosystem—of all the start-ups that were developing software for the personal computer revolution. PeopleSoft was the first to build human resources (HR) software from the ground up for this new corporate computing environment. They were going to change the way people processed data, and I was going to make their Payroll software look sexy.

In 1991, PeopleSoft was small, but their conference room was enormous and impressively appointed with a black granite conference table so smooth and glossy you could see your own reflection. Sunlight poured in through the floor-to-ceiling windows along one wall. I planted myself at the far end of the table in front of a big screen, ready to deal out each of my overheads, one after the other, on the glass bed of their projector. The executives trooped in, arranging themselves at the end of the table, creating between us a vast, vacant, obsidian no-man's-land. They were all older and much more experienced. But I was ready for them.

DISARM FEAR

I was focused on answering one question: How was I going to help their company? It was on me to reveal *their* needs to *them* and to show how *my* approach would exceed *their* expectations.

Was I about to fake it on my way toward making it?

Honestly, there were moments I was anxious enough to say to myself, *Who am I kidding? This is nuts. They won't take me seriously, so I better make something up to sell them on me.* But as I went through the process of preparing, I became more and more confident. It was all about finding and knowing the right information and being secure in that knowledge. I disarmed my fear. There was, in fact, no need to fake it.

There was no BS in my pitch. It was all about having insights about *them* that *they* didn't even know about themselves. I had researched everything I could find to learn about PeopleSoft's business, technology, and competition, and I thought deeply about the strategies and tactics the company needed. My proposal was all about being genuinely passionate about *them* and crafting the approach that fit *them*—perfectly.

I presented Sabrina Horn Public Relations as a boutique offering a high-quality service that was thoroughly plugged into the Silicon Valley tech ecosystem. A start-up like PeopleSoft, on its way up, required a partner like me, not a vendor that had to be told what to do. I told them how they would be my first marquee client and how I would grow my practice. I shared how I would outsource certain functions to manage my overhead and avoid passing unnecessary expenses on to them.

Pulling from my business plan, I detailed for them how I would be different. PeopleSoft urgently needed help telling a complicated story. They needed a new PR approach, to push and pull their prospects to them. In 1991, tech PR was primarily a tactical marketing function focused on grinding out press releases and pitching to reporters story ideas that might get written up in a computer magazine. It was more cost-effective and credible than advertising because it was unbiased news coverage written by a third party, as opposed to ad copy designed, controlled, and paid for by a company with a big budget. Anyway, it wasn't very sophisticated, and in all of Silicon Valley, probably less than a handful of PR firms were considered strategic.

For PeopleSoft, I created a "rolling thunder" series of programs that would build on each other, one in anticipation of the next, to raise the company's profile. And then I threw in big, creative ideas they could grow into, just to show them I could think outside the box. My value proposition would help PeopleSoft cut through the noise and build their brand with a more personal, thoughtful, and integrated approach to communications.

Part of my preparation involved writing down every single question they might ask, and more importantly, every objection they might raise. I found the answers. As soon as I found them all, I asked myself what I had missed. Starting out as a one-woman band, I had to be firm and realistic about the extent of what I could do. For example, when one of Dave's executives asked if I could handle investor relations, a highly specialized form of PR dealing with shareholder and financial communications, I said no, adding that I could recommend other investor relations firms I knew and, as was the practice in my industry at that time, would happily partner with. When another exec asked me if I could get the company a story in *Business Week* (now *Bloomberg Businessweek*), I did not eagerly shout, "Sure!" Instead, I responded, "Very likely. But here's what it will take to make that happen." Promising too much would have been grossly exaggerating the truth and setting up them and myself for major disappointment.

When you are first starting out, doing and being anything to win the business is tempting—and also dangerous. You have to be bullish and yet stay grounded in the reality of what your company can realistically do, and then target those customers that want what you have to offer, with relatively few modifications.

Next, I made it my business to find out who my competition would be. No matter how big or experienced the other bidders were, I had the upstart mojo of the underdog. I would position my company's turn-on-a-dime start-up agility in contrast to everyone else's establishment approach. For me, having no company and no employees but more enthusiasm and passion than any competitor was a differentiator.

Throughout the entire pitch, I remained acutely aware of McGlinchey & Paul, my rival, a tech agency out of Boston. Dick McGlinchey knew PeopleSoft's VP of Sales, who happened to be the CEO's brother. They already had the account for Lotus, a white-hot software company in the late 1980s and early 1990s. McGlinchey had brought a small army of account execs to its PeopleSoft pitch. More threatening, however, was all the schwag littering the conference table: pads and pens and mugs boasting the McGlinchey logo. I touched one of those hefty pens and felt a shiver of doom.

Driving home, I did not second-guess myself. There would always be competition. I had truly done my very best. Two hours later, checking my messages, I heard the voice of Linda Zecher, then PeopleSoft's VP of Marketing.

"Good news . . ." she began.

Dave Duffield and his team had decided to give me a chance, perhaps identifying with my passion for their company and my entrepreneurial spirit, thoroughness, candor, and creativity. I won the business—$7,000 a month, which comes to a little more than $13,000 in today's dollars, a very respectable PR budget. My emotions were mixed, something between total elation and abject fear.

I saved the call to my parents for later that night, and I was glad I did, because my father did not react as I thought he would.

"I DON'T THINK YOU CAN DO THIS"

He spoke with no emotion at all.

"Sabrina, I don't think you can do this."

Speechless, I nevertheless managed to ask, "Why?"

"You don't have an MBA, you can't balance your own checkbook, and you've never run a company," said my father, by now an experienced VC. He further elaborated on how I didn't have the acumen of Bill Gates, who was well on his way to changing the world.

For the record, he was right on all counts. Nevertheless, I had single-handedly won a very viable client based on my own expertise, against tough competition. I was controlling my own destiny and I was "making it." And now the man who had instilled in me this very ethos didn't believe in me? I was devastated.

The next day, I quickly started to regroup. On my way to work, I realized that being Bill Gates was not a prerequisite for claiming a place in the tech sector. I was not *making* technology but offering a valuable *service* to help companies market their technologies. I had a much better than average set of the necessary skills. Moreover, I had an original perspective on applying them to a new wave of software companies on the horizon. I knew I was going to be among the very first to catch that wave.

Being both ambitious *and* realistic, I told myself, *If I don't do this, I will never know if I could have been successful. If I fail? My ability to make a living will not come to an end. I can always get a job somewhere, working for someone. Right?*

The realization that I could fail but still go on earning a living was very empowering, liberating, and fundamental in organizing my risk. I knew that, either way, I would ultimately be okay.

ORGANIZE RISK

What's the worst that could happen? I asked myself. In any venture, risk is real and cannot be ignored. But fear of risk is itself a risk, which can sink you before you even begin. Allow yourself to be swamped by that anxious, frustrated, and fearful feeling and it will cloud your ability to move forward.

As an entrepreneur and a future founder, it is this fear—the fear of failing and of the unknown—that can be so overwhelming as to make you want to stick your head in the sand even as you lose your footing. The antidote? For me, it was revisiting my capabilities and skill set, staring down the fear, and, in a sense, reassuring myself that I could indeed do this, that I had a better than even chance of success, and that whatever I was confronted with, I would find the resources to handle it. To put it another way, I was organizing the risk.

For me, organizing risk began on a micro scale. I needed to make sure that, whatever happened, I could do my part to pay the mortgage and the bills. I realized that I had remarkably little to lose. I had no responsibility other than to my one client, to myself, and to my husband, who was very supportive of my entrepreneurial aspirations. Our marriage, sadly, didn't last in the long run, but we were very much a team at the time, solving problems together. This was tremendously comforting and helpful, though not everyone has the kind of built-in positive support system I had starting out. A new venture is a stress test for any relationship. From the get-go, you need to know where you stand, and if the support is not there, you had better come to grips with it or get to work developing it.

Unlike a product business, my company was a service business in which the product—at least initially—was only me. I had very few operating expenses, and at that stage I didn't even need an office. Had I chosen to start a different kind of business, taken a loan, filed for patents, and incurred other costs, the risks would have been on a completely different level.

There was one more important risk factor, though. I did not want to burn any bridges. Starting my company meant leaving my current employer. There were issues like noncompete agreements to consider. Two days after I won my first account, I met with my two bosses, Maureen Blanc and Simone Otus, the founders of their eponymous firm Blanc & Otus, one of the top tech agencies in the United States. I had no ax to grind, and they had been good to me. Because I won my first account on their watch, I had to do the right thing.

I took a calculated gamble. I told them what I had gone out and done, and why. They certainly weren't thrilled with my news, but as entrepreneurs themselves, they knew that I had to do what was burning inside me. If I hadn't done it then, I would have done it soon. My aspirations at that time were limited: a small shop with maybe a handful of employees. I also knew my newly won account was too small for them and that they weren't interested in business application software clients at the time.

There was little overlap. They gave me their blessing and wished me luck.

When you leave your employer to start something on your own or to join another company, really try do it on good terms and don't bite the hand that fed you. Of course, that's not always possible, given personalities, competitive issues, intellectual property, and other legal matters, but it's still an important aspiration. Reputation matters, and what goes around, comes around. For as long as I was in business, I upheld my promise that I would never intentionally recruit Blanc & Otus's people or clients. We are still good friends today, and I treasure that. Remember this: on your own, you will be doing business tomorrow with yesterday's network. Keep it positive. Make it work. Frame *your* move so that those in your network have some kind of stake, and never burn your old bosses, colleagues, or clients.

The last bridge I refused to burn was the one between my father and me. Despite the doubt he expressed, he offered me a desk in his own company's office in Cupertino. I gratefully accepted. My first day in business was June 4, 1991.

In retrospect, there was tremendous value in my father's doubt. It made me make damn sure that I wasn't faking *anything*. I tapped into those survival instincts, reconfirmed my strategy, and doubled down on my resolve. I could indeed do this. I would not give up. I would make my first client delighted they had chosen me. In addition, I would prove to my parents that I could be successful on my own terms—something my father proudly conceded, some five years later.

I would make it.

BUILD STRUCTURE

When you have a business making products, you want the best manufacturing. When your product is people, you want the best talent. Regardless of business type, most companies start by first assembling an accomplished executive team to secure financing. But I didn't need outside money because I was bootstrapping my business, funding it with the revenue from my clients. All I needed was a team to service those accounts and get the work done.

My first employee checked all the boxes. I hired him, my husband and I assembled his desk, and, silly as it was, I even sharpened his pencils—because I wanted everything to be perfect for him on his first day. And so it was—for a couple weeks. Then I began to feel he just wasn't into it, or into me, or into our clients. Sadly, I realized he wasn't going to last when I saw his updated résumé sitting on his desk.

He—my first employee—left after one month!

Intellectually, I understood. He wanted to work in the consumer industry, not B2B tech. But personally, I was crushed. I learned two hard lessons here. First, for the foreseeable future, I would only hire people who had experience and interest in the market on which my company was focused. Second, as a founder, I realized that nobody would ever love my business as much as I did. This was the start of learning not to take business matters personally.

My second employee, Annette Shimada, was perfect for what the business needed at that time. She was the "total package," could do a little bit of everything, and had a strong work ethic. I first engaged her on a freelance basis and then brought her on full time. This was a hedging strategy. Next came Marilyn Callaghan, who fit in between me and Annette. She could help me win and support more clients. She became my first director, the start of a leadership team. I slowly added other employees, at both senior and middle levels, and according to technology experience and skill set, to help support the clients we won.

Within three months, we had moved to an executive office suite space in Burlingame, closer to San Francisco and near the airport. Like the incubators of today, this facility had shared administrative services, providing relief from things like billing and invoicing, answering phones, or copying, faxing, and mailing documents—all of which were manual tasks then. At some point in your company's growth, you may find your own space, but in the beginning it is more efficient to distribute the load. The more tightly you can control discretionary spending, the less you will need to scramble just to pay near-term bills. Such prudence goes a long way toward reducing stress and any resulting impulse to fake it.

Indeed, I was financially disciplined. I adhered to a very rudimentary principle that worked until our business grew and became more complex. It was my 30/30/40 rule. For every dollar we made, we put away 30% for Uncle Sam, saved another 30% to reinvest in the business and build a cash cushion, leaving 40% for everything else: payroll, rent, and other stuff. For a service business with fairly basic needs, 30/30/40 was all the financial management we needed. Your ratios will differ, and business is much more complicated today than it was in 1991, but my point is to know what those ratios are and to manage to them. I watched those numbers like a hawk until I could hire a finance director.

Financial discipline also meant having the chutzpah to ask my clients to pay their bills. I learned the truth about the phrase "The check's in the mail." The real truth is, you don't have the money until *their* check has cleared *your* bank. For a long time, I handled those collection calls personally. Moreover, I wanted my staff to see me doing it. "Every dollar counts, always," I told them. An unpaid bill for $57.23 was money to take them out for drinks after a long, busy week.

At first my company was a sole proprietorship with salaried and bonused employees. In our second year, we became an S corporation, and we eventually added equity ownership plans to retain and incentivize my growing leadership team. This would be very important when competing for talent, particularly in the land of option-filled, venture-backed Silicon Valley start-ups.

I moved forward step by step, always taking care to mind my footing. Keeping your feet on the ground and maintaining continuous contact with reality, you will find fewer reasons to question or doubt yourself. And that means you will find that you have no need to fake anything.

TOO MUCH BUSINESS

To say that PeopleSoft became a successful company is an understatement. Going public on NASDAQ only eighteen months after becoming my client, with a market cap of $7 billion, they were the hot, high-profile company of that time, in effect changing the enterprise software industry. Our work helped create and bring their story to life, and we put their name up in lights. We never felt like we worked *for* them. We were a part of them and worked *with* them to help make them successful, a personalized partnering approach that became a key to our client service. And their success became our success. It turned out that many tech companies that partnered with PeopleSoft for their technology also wanted access to PeopleSoft's PR firm. Companies heard about us. Our work spoke for itself. It was like shooting fish in a barrel.

"Too much business" is one of those things for which you won't find much sympathy. "That's what we call a good problem to have," people will tell you. In fact, I soon realized that there are thresholds beyond which it is simply impossible for x number of people to deliver great service to y number of customers. This kind of thing was (and still is) a common story among many agencies, and it was a painful revelation in my own shop.

"We have to keep the wheels from coming off the bus," said Marilyn. When too much business comes too early along your growth curve and you can't scale with it at the same pace, you have a capacity problem. Morale declines, quality ebbs, results suffer, and overnight your hard-earned high-end reputation can change to low quality, careless, and cookie cutter. You are faking it.

I quickly developed a sense for how much revenue and how many clients to apportion per person and per team based on requirements and skill sets. Matching my resources to the ebb and flow of business was both science and art: a delicate balance between the three vectors of people, money, and time. Having fewer but bigger clients was a lot better than having lots of little clients. We decided to turn away smaller prospects, referring them to other trusted firms. We became more selective with companies that approached us. I established vetting criteria, including the quality of a prospect's leadership team and financial backers, the clarity of their vision, size, market opportunity, and other factors. We raised our minimum retainer and, over time, moved away from a blended hourly rate to variable rates by seniority and skill.

I also started deploying what I called the Hamburger Helper solution. A Betty Crocker product, around since 1971, Hamburger Helper is basically a box of dried pasta and powdered seasonings that you combine with browned ground beef. It's not something you want to eat every day, but it works in a pinch and is an economical way of extending your ground beef. My Hamburger Helpers were freelancers and contractors, a variable workforce we could activate during peak periods. This is a common practice in today's gig economy, but it was still novel in the early 1990s.

ARE YOU READY?

It was during our first year of business that I gained a greater appreciation for what it really means to be a founder. Starting a company is actually quite transactional, like a moment in time with a beginning, a middle, and an end. You do a lot of work in preparation: writing your business plan, developing your initial product or service offering, getting funding, winning your first customer, getting a bank account, filing papers . . . and then one day you are officially in business!

It is then that the real work begins. Being a true founder is a position without boundaries but with infinite responsibilities. Every day, I was innovating new ideas and processes, "founding" new ways to be efficient and deliver results, interact with clients, stay on top of trends, and build our reputation. I had less than a handful of employees and clients, but I was managing them and leading them. I was laying down the foundation on which to grow a successful long-term business. It was all-consuming, exhilarating, exhausting, and at times overwhelming.

I cannot say that, before I started my company, I asked myself if I was ready to be a founder. Of course, I had never before founded a company or had any kind of leadership training, so how could I know what to be ready for?

I had *watched* others—my father, my former bosses Maureen and Simone, previous clients, and well-known executives in the industry. All I knew at the time was that I wanted to control my destiny and I had a Big Idea. I accepted that I would have to work incredibly hard and that it wouldn't always be a rosy picture. I have never regretted my decision, but there were moments when my inexperience frustrated me and when I considered taking shortcuts to avoid working so hard and to move faster.

To spare yourself some of those moments of frustration and doubt, I advise you to ask the question *Am I ready to be a founder?*

While you ponder that, also consider exactly what role you might play within your company. If this sounds obvious, the reality is that this consideration is one most often overlooked. Most entrepreneurs are so thoroughly consumed with their Big Idea that the *reality* of actually running a company day to day, let alone understanding their own role as a founder, has yet to cross their minds.

For example, some founders are also CEOs of their start-ups—but only to a certain stage of growth. At some point, they step aside to bring in someone more experienced, or worse, their investors do it for them. Others assume different positions, such as chief technology officer or head of business development and sales. My point is that starting a company doesn't mean you *must* run it, too. You can divide and conquer by joining forces with a partner or other individuals who share in your vision. But all this requires careful forethought, something I talk more about in chapter 9, "The Founder's Curse."

For now, do yourself a favor. Inventory yourself and do some introspective thinking. Align different roles and jobs with your own experience and skill set.

- What functions and tasks are you good at? In which are you lacking? Consider your past professional experience and contrast strengths with weaknesses. For example, I am good at coming up with new ideas and finding solutions to problems, but I lack the patience to implement those solutions.

- What do you love doing, and what tasks are like fingernails on a chalkboard for you? I love thinking about what is possible, getting people excited about that, and connecting people who would otherwise have no reason to meet. I can't stand corporate politics, red tape, or too much process.

- Aside from "founder," which job title do you envision having within your company? Take a few minutes and research that title. Do you meet the criteria for that job description? Where do you fall short? Who would you need to complement you?

Answering these questions and seeking out people you trust for their honest feedback are the first steps in assigning yourself the right job. Getting the answer right is really your first act of leadership. With this in hand, you will have a much clearer sense of the team you need to build around you. It will enable you to execute more efficiently, so that you will encounter fewer problems that need solving. Most important, by grounding yourself in reality, you will avoid getting in over your head, making mistakes, potentially faking it, and then squandering precious time cleaning up after yourself.

FOUNDING VALUES

As a founder or a CEO, you have a unique opportunity—and responsibility—to set the values for your organization.

Why is this so important to do now? Why can't you just get started and figure it out later?

Because values are the foundation for about half of the reputation of the company you intend to start and likely will determine 44% of its market value.[1] Values will be the basis of your company's brand, your culture and traditions, what you stand for, how your people behave and perform, how you work and communicate, and everything in between. The right value system will keep you and your people in line. It can protect you from taking the shortcuts that sabotage early business success.

I discuss setting core values as essential to brand creation in chapter 4, "Becoming and Staying an Authentic Brand." I also highly recommend reading *What You Do Is Who You Are: How to Create Your Business Culture* by Ben Horowitz, famous tech VC, serial founder, and CEO. Here, though, it is important to point out that many entrepreneurs fail, at the very outset, to devote sufficient thought to their company values because they are simply too busy doing other things, like building product or raising money. In fact, if you ask the typical person working at the typical start-up, they will tell you their company values are defined by Thirsty Thursdays, free snacks, and a "mission statement" posted above the front door.

This is not what I mean by establishing a values-based culture.

A lack of a strong company value system can cause more HR nightmares than you ever imagined. Values are also important to establish at the outset, so others in your company don't plant the seeds for the wrong ones. Fixing a dysfunctional culture is much more difficult than creating a brand-new one.

Thus, for the privilege of being a founder with a Big Idea, you must undertake *this* exercise at *this* time. A great business plan should contain a list of core values. It's okay to keep them simple and limited to a few when you first start out. They should be a reflection of you, in combination with the inherent purpose of your business. There will be plenty of time to expand upon them as your business grows, and there are plenty of templates and guidelines to help you think that through. And, yes, you need to be ready to lead by example and to live up to those values in every way. Every. Single. Day.

Know that you will be under a microscope. You are establishing the ground rules and you will be watched—from the smallest gesture, like putting your coffee cup in the company dishwasher (not the sink), to the most consequential decisions, like firing your highest-paying client because he is an asshole to your staff. As a leader, people will look up to you. Some will want to be like you. They will copy you. And they will be quick to remind you when you stray from the standards you *yourself* established for them.

Still want to start a company?

DISARM FEAR, ORGANIZE RISK

Starting any company or new venture presents risks. You will be faced with the unknown, which can cause uncertainty and fear. As you curl your toes over the edge of the cliff, getting ready to jump, you may think, *I don't know everything. Maybe I know very little. Faking it sure is tempting. And faking it may be the only way.* But "faking it" is basically the same thing as lying, and this is definitely not a value with which you want to launch a business.

As the twenty-nine-year-old founder of a company, with no prior business management experience, I had many opportunities to fake it. "Acting as if" would only take me so far. There comes a point where a person either knows what to do and can muster the confidence to go out there and do it or decides that being an entrepreneur is just not a good fit.

DISARM FEAR, ORGANIZE RISK

☐ Identify and ingrain your inspiration.

☐ Never lose sight of your value proposition and business purpose.

☐ Seek information to turn the unknown into the known.

☐ Ask yourself the toughest questions and answer them. (Be very clear with yourself on the limits of your offering and capabilities.)

☐ Identify your risks and label them: financial, operational, engineering, sales, and so on.

☐ Understand your worst-case scenario for each risk, and then identify what is worse than that.

☐ Clearly understand how you will make ends meet and recover (loans, mortgages, contracts, obligations, other liabilities).

☐ Make sure your business model and how you will make money are rock solid and ironclad.

☐ Consider and preserve key relationships in your personal and professional network.

☐ Defray costs with technology and temporary solutions.

☐ Find leaders who complement you and identify with your business purpose.

☐ Identify your role and essential core values.

I beat back virtually every temptation to fake it with a clear strategy and an ironclad set of tactics for launching my business. The essence of my business plan was my platform, my positioning, and I would stay laser-focused on this, sticking only to what I knew. In this way, I eliminated the FUD factor: the fear, uncertainty, and doubt that fuel the engine of fakery.

Throughout my career, whenever I was facing a crisis or felt rudderless, I attacked fear, uncertainty, and doubt and any stirrings of the imposter syndrome by referring to factual reality. I sought information to develop new strategies and options. It was my survival instinct kicking in, deftly defusing the bombs that running a business can drop in your lap. On that basis, I took comfort in knowing that I never actually needed to fake it. Somewhere out there, I would reason with myself, there would always be a solution to whatever problem I was dealing with. Like a detective, I just had to find it, or piece it together. I knew that the answer I needed and the decision I needed to make, as complex and hidden as they might be, were within reach. This self-knowledge saved me countless times over the years.

Two years into running my business, I recognized an especially challenging (and daunting) reality. With a handful of us now serving seven or eight clients, I was the owner of a viable business, an expert firm with a growing reputation. More clients were on the horizon. I should have been ecstatic. Instead, I had butterflies in my gut. It hit me: I would lose those clients—and more—if I didn't scale and grow. This reality shock was an inflection point, not just for me but for my company.

It was time, then, to change the journey. There was no option in the middle. To stay the same actually meant decline. Gaining altitude meant becoming the leader of a real company and a CEO, not just a passionate entrepreneur and the anxious manager of a team.

CHAPTER THREE

BECOMING A CEO

You may be reading this book because you want to start your own company or you aspire to be the CEO of an existing business. Maybe you already are the CEO of your organization or you want to move up the corporate ladder to a top position. Or maybe you just want to understand your boss better. Regardless of your current job and professional goals, it is to your great advantage to understand leadership from the perspective of the chief executive officer. CEO is the ultimate position of power and leadership in business. To think about leadership, start from the top.

STEP IT UP, OR STEP OUT

Founding a business calls for one set of leadership skills. Moving from launch to early growth and then expansion requires another. Somewhere around two years into starting my company, we reached an inflection point. Our clients wanted to know if we could scale with them, provide more senior talent on their teams, and offer certain specialized services they would need down the line. They also wanted a firm that was a real industry player, that could bring to the table a broader network of relationships and influence.

The writing was on the wall. If I didn't grow, I would lose the clients I had, along with my employees and any chance of being something more than a little shop. What's more, I needed to offer benefits like health insurance and institute proper HR policies for my existing employees. We had outgrown the temporary office facilities and needed our own space. So I signed a five-year, multimillion-dollar lease with my personal guarantee. *That* was sobering.

Staying the same size, which is a viable strategy for many small businesses, wasn't an option for me. But stepping up my game meant taking on new levels of responsibility, for which I had even fewer skills than when I first started out. It meant expanding my range from a PR pro to a savvy, strategic businesswoman, and growing into a person of industry repute. Growth also carried with it the potential for a whole new level of mistakes and, yes, opportunities to fake it.

I put "CEO" on my business card when we became an S corporation and changed our name from Sabrina Horn Public Relations to Horn Group. These steps were at once gratifying, motivating, and humbling. Around me, men and (a few) women with the same title—all with a lot more experience than I—were running huge global corporations. They had earned the title and had *become* CEOs. I felt I had a really long way to go and a lot to live up to.

What I came to learn, though—and it may be of some relief to you—is that a CEO is always *becoming* a CEO. Even the best, most experienced chief executives know they are perpetually arriving—learning, solving new problems, and earning their title—every day. In fact, I felt that if I actually ever "arrived" or "made it," I would need to quit my job. Why? Because you're always making it as a CEO, ready for battle, anticipating your next move, and keeping your edge. And let me tell you, there's nothing to keep your edge like going to work every day, bobbing and weaving, wondering what you're going to have to deal with. CEOs have to navigate new unknowns daily while still steering the ship forward.

This was the beginning of real growth—both personally for me and for my company—from founding a business and having the *incumbent* authority to run it, to growing a business and having the *legitimate* authority to lead it. Legitimacy must be earned daily from your company's stakeholders: customers, employees, investors, vendors, partners, advisors, and the media.

And growth is wonderful. It creates opportunity on many levels. It makes the rain go away, the clouds part, and the sun come out. But growth also creates change and, with it, challenges. (They don't call them "growing pains" for nothing.) CEOs must lead through change and achieve growth while navigating over or around every obstacle along the way *and* staying true to core values and beliefs.

YOUR RESULTS MAY VARY

Being a new CEO, I read lots of books on leadership and looked to others for advice. I began to feel, however, like I was buying a weight-loss product or an investment offer. I appreciated the fine-print warning: "Your results may vary." What increasingly mattered to me was looking within, at what leadership "traits" *I* possessed. I needed to know what was important to *me* and to assess the values and qualities *I* stood for. All of this had to be based on the present, not on who I wanted to be or what I wanted others to think of me.

So just what are the personality characteristics of a leader? Here is my list of attributes and insights, the things that matter to me. I think they are applicable to anyone, in any kind of leadership role, but use them to help you figure out what's relevant to you and to your current position, business, and industry. Your results may vary.

20/20 Vision

Every successful leader creates goals. They are visions of a desired future state. Yet they must not deny present reality. Improvement and growth can never rely on faking it until you make it. Every step toward a desired future state must be taken within an ever-changing state of reality. Facing reality can be brutal and disappointing, especially when you have to admit your own mistakes. But it is vitally important to maintain a hard sense of reality and an unshakable respect for that reality at all times. It is the basis for every decision you make.

Optimism Never Gives Up

Optimism is an umbrella for being strategic, forward-thinking, positive, ambitious, and visionary. Optimism drives enthusiasm, without which, I am convinced, nothing great can be accomplished. Is it possible to be "unrealistically" optimistic and "wildly" enthusiastic? Yes, any quality divorced from reality is dangerous. But trading optimism for pessimism, or enthusiasm for timidity, is a disastrous bargain. Optimistic leaders look for solutions at all times, often when the stakes are highest, at the darkest moments, at the eleventh hour. They search for a way out or a loophole to find a way in. They want to keep moving forward somehow, and the knowledge that there is always a better way keeps them from giving up. Who wouldn't want that person in their foxhole? Yes, optimistic leaders must be grounded in reality, but their tireless ability to push forward is inspiring, and quite often it is what separates the winners from the losers in business.

Integrity

Integrity is the table stakes for leadership. To possess integrity, you need to be whole, undivided, sound, uncorrupted, and incorruptible. Engineers and architects speak of "structural integrity," meaning the ability of a structure or structural component to hold together, under a load, without breaking or getting bent out of shape. A leader with integrity is unbreakable. Integrity is also your number one antidote to faking it. It will keep you honest and it will quickly identify those who are not. In just one small example, within our company, leading with integrity meant being able to have difficult conversations with clients and employees about uncomfortable subjects like money and performance. It's up to you as the leader to lead by example and to make it okay for everyone to be honest. Holding back reality, or the truth, is just another method of faking it, and it ultimately holds the entire organization back.

Know What You Don't Know

Being humble may not seem like an obvious CEO trait. You'd be hard pressed to find a leader who lacked self-esteem or had a sense of unworthiness. But the best leaders do have a realistic appreciation of their strengths and weaknesses. They are secure in knowing that they don't know everything, and they have no problem asking for help, learning from others, even apologizing for their mistakes. That level of confidence draws people in. Humility drives open-mindedness and keeps you hungry for knowledge, facts, and data—the very elements of reality. Humility, like integrity, is a strong arrow in the anti-faker's quiver.

Resilience and Commitment

I used to joke with my employees about the days I'd put on my Wonder Woman cuffs while commuting into what I knew would be a tough day at the office. It was really a metaphor for what I would face, repelling whatever came at me, protecting my company and my clients, and going on to live another day.

Every leader develops something of a thick skin, and being resilient is the key to bouncing back after the hits they inevitably take. You've heard the saying "What doesn't kill you makes you stronger." Well, it's true. You learn to manage the fallout,

continuing to lead through the setbacks, and then rebound—
better for the experience. Resilience is built by leading through
the countless problems that land in your lap and also by
enduring prolonged periods of difficulty. The point is, as a CEO,
you have to stand up to hard times. You cannot give up. You
have to persevere. There are no shortcuts. That level of commitment and dedication is not for everybody, but it is an absolute
requirement for the job, and for success.

It's What You Say and How You Say It

There is nothing less inspiring than listening to a boring,
ineffective speaker. Being a leader, you need to engage with a
variety of stakeholders at different levels, often communicating
difficult and complicated messages in periods of crisis. Being
charismatic and a good communicator is always helpful, in any
situation. Presence and communication are acquired skills that
require practice and coaching. Also, bear in mind that practical
information, especially complex news and big changes, must
be explained multiple times through different channels until
your audience truly understands. Frequency is important in
comprehension.

Adapt Early, Move Quickly

Procrastination is one of the CEO's worst enemies. Yet, as a
leader, you won't always have complete information or enough
time to make a fully informed decision. Sometimes you just
have to wrap your head around what is happening and go with
the safest, most viable option based on what you know at that
particular moment. You might even make the wrong decision.
Yet the wrong move can sometimes be better than no move at
all.[1] Slow decision makers become bottlenecks, and their teams
get frustrated, causing them to lose faith in their leader.

For example, if you think you might need to lay people off
because a downturn may be approaching in your sector, don't
wait to hear about it on the news. If that noise is out there,

it's likely happening, and you're already late. It is critical to be flexible and adapt your business quickly, whether to new technologies on the horizon or, as we have seen more recently, to events such as a global pandemic. See reality for what it is, adapt as soon as you can, make your move expeditiously and with conviction.

Intuition Is Knowledge, and Knowledge Is Intuition

A lot has been said about intuition as a secret sauce in leadership success. I may have a contrarian view about intuition in that I don't believe it is a sixth sense that we work to develop. Human intuition is just knowledge, tidbits of information, observations, mental notes, and past slivers of experience that we have accumulated over time. This knowledge is triggered and recalled to be helpful in certain situations. That "gut feel" gets stronger as we get older and accumulate more knowledge over time. We know what to do because we have a substantial body of data somewhere in our consciousness.

My point is not to argue over whether intuition exists. You already have the knowledge, the common sense, and the inductive reasoning skills to handle most of the challenges and decisions you must make as a CEO. You need to trust that knowledge and have confidence in it, not fake it with a pseudo solution that fails to address the issue at hand.

You may build some of these traits and others into your leadership approach, but remember, they are all interrelated. You can be as honest as the day is long but miss your revenue targets. You can move too quickly under pressure and choose the wrong investor. You can come across as grossly uninformed in your quest for information and naive in your unbridled enthusiasm for your business. Everything lies in the levers you have to use in any given situation, which will be uniquely different from the next situation. The important thing here is that you identify the levers, label them, and rely on them as you form your personal leadership style. When you know your leadership levers—your particular strengths—play to them consistently. Put them on display. Let everyone see your leadership skills and attributes in action. Everything you say or do should seem purposeful. Nothing should appear superfluous or, even worse, random.

CEO OJT

It was a typical day. I was finalizing the details of a new work-from-home policy with HR, strategizing with my partner on how to boost revenue in San Francisco, and reviewing our new digital services offering. That morning, Jim, a senior employee, asked me for a huge raise because he had received an offer from a competitor. Giving him what he wanted would throw off our entire pay scale and piss off his peers (which would cause a whole other problem). Turning him down would put a major account in jeopardy, if he decided to leave.

In general, I was worried about our bottom line and was counting on having a good year to reinvest in the business and modernize our information technology (IT) infrastructure. I had to make some kind of progress on each one of these fronts *today*, tweaking here, asking for more information there, keeping the goal in mind, making decisions one way or the other. No one taught me how to handle any of these situations or how to approach making the necessary decisions. I learned by doing them, on the job.

In the case of Jim, I played to his desire for more money and stature by giving him substantially greater earning potential through his bonus—not a raise—and the opportunity to work with me on a special project. Even if he accepted, I now figured he wouldn't be long for my world, and I immediately set in motion a plan to replace him. He stayed for six months, and the steps I took preserved not only our salary structure but also continuity of service for my client, on *my* terms. I learned not to let anybody put me on the horns of *their* dilemma—in this case, Jim's binary offer. I offered a third way, which gave me back some control.

How did I know what to do? On-the-job training (OJT), right then and there.

As I was leaving the office that day, one of my employees said, "Hey, Sab, what's bugging you so much? You're the CEO! You can do whatever you want!"

Two thoughts came to mind.

One: *You are not helping.*

Two: *You will never be a CEO.*

Many people misunderstand the role of the CEO. The disconnect starts with an unrealistic stereotype of a charismatic six-foot-tall white man with a degree from a top university. He is a natural-born leader with a direct-to-the-top career path, endless amounts of money, and an effortless ability to make perfect decisions under pressure.[2]

The truth is, most successful CEOs have made many costly mistakes on their journey to the top, they often are introverts, and they don't have an Ivy League pedigree.[3] There also is more diversity at the top these days—although still far from enough. Regardless of gender, race, education, or station in life, most CEOs work their way up the corporate ladder for years, learn from their CEO or from leaders of other companies, gradually take on more responsibility, run a business unit capable of producing either a profit or a loss, then more P&Ls, and ultimately step into the top role themselves.

Still others, like yours truly, become CEOs by starting their own businesses, often with little to no management experience. In retrospect, I definitely could have benefited from a few more years of grooming, as it would have given me more experience and confidence, enabling me to avoid certain mistakes. Then again, I probably would have missed the tech wave I used to launch my business. Timing is everything, and business is a series of trade-offs—in time.

The hard truth is that no matter how much schooling you have, how much sub-CEO management experience you have, or how many CEO shoulders you have looked over, nothing can adequately prepare you for the top job. Even serial CEOs know that their job will be different in each company they run. The only comprehensive training for the top job can be spelled out in six initials: CEO OJT. You learn the role by playing it, in real time. You *do* the job.

LEARNING TO LEAD

Some people might smirk and think, *Yeah, on-the-job training is just a fancy type of faking it till you make it.* Superficially, this may be the case. My experience, however, is that there is a world of difference between doing *your* best and *pretending* that you are doing *the* best. I have always tried to do my best, and I continually measured the results of my efforts against outcomes. My intention was to continually close the quality gap between my best effort and what it produced. In this way, OJT produced incremental improvement. But I never deceived myself that *my* best was *the* best. That would have been faking it.

The essence of on-the-job training for leadership is in the act of decision-making: identifying, understanding, strategizing, planning, discussing, prioritizing, weighing, implementing, and correcting decisions. Learning how to make the right decisions at the right time is the mark of a great CEO and a predictor of long-term business success.

Whether you are new to the role or are a more experienced leader, it can be easy to lose your way, yield to pressure, and act when you have no idea what to do. Sometimes you think you see a way to mitigate a situation with a short-term fix. Sometimes you shove a big problem under the rug in the hope of buying time to sort things out. These are all decisions to delay the necessary *ultimate* decision. Tactics aimed at easing the discomfort of the moment almost always end up creating greater pain in the longer term.

Instead of faking it in the hope of buying time to make it, find the time now to differentiate the imagined from the real. Study the immediate situation, assess the problem's character- istics, its causes and effects, and formulate viable responses. Confer with well-informed, levelheaded people you trust.

KEEP A LEVEL HEAD AND A STEADY HAND

Often, problems will be presented to you by people under duress. The drama and anxiety of these situations can be great. It's easy to get sucked in, and you may feel compelled to act right away. Take a breath. Stay neutral and calm. Listen carefully, ask questions, validate facts, understand consequences, and put the situation in context. You don't want to overreact or to solve one problem only to create two others. Action may, in fact, need to be taken urgently—but perhaps in a different way than is at first apparent or, as is often the case, in a phased approach.

Emotionally based decisions are usually the wrong decisions. At a minimum, they are almost always poorly executed. Keep emotions as well as emotional people at bay and out of the decision-making process.

The great thing I learned about business problems is that, unlike personal problems, they are frequently black and white. Their solutions have a clear financial impact, which is either green or red. Often—not always—the answers are hiding in plain sight, in the numbers. And often—but not always—if they are seen as financial decisions, they can be the easiest to make. Of course, sometimes the financial implications of a decision are secondary and you have no choice but to bite the bullet and do the right thing, such as investing in socially distant outdoor seating or repairing your faulty product.

There is also simply and finally the need to just be pragmatic in business, which means making decisions that cut corners for the sake of efficiency, without sacrificing safety or value. You want to deliver value for value received, you want all stakeholders to benefit, you want to act lawfully and to follow your inner moral compass, but you know that if you fail to be pragmatic and move quickly, you risk losing your competitive edge. Knowing when to cut corners requires informed leadership. There is a litmus test to guide these kinds of decisions. The difference between pragmatism and faking it is the absence of an intent to deceive. Once again, that is the bright red line.

So, gather all the information you need, ask yourself if there is anything else you *don't* see, and then examine all your options. Make a decision that solves the problem and creates the greatest good for the whole organization. Decisions made in this way are informed and calculated. And they deserve your confidence.

A SHORT COURSE ON HUMILITY

Pop culture depicts the CEO as the woman or man with all the answers. In the real world, the CEO is a person who has all the questions and the confidence to ask them.

For me, humility is inextricably linked to openness, curiosity, and a mindset that is receptive to learning. Humility prevents you from faking it. It gives you so much power. It nudges you to double-check, to get confirmation, to give a second thought to the most important decisions you make. When confronted with an unknown, the curious CEO will find the information needed before deciding how to proceed. In contrast, the faker CEO never admits ignorance, uncertainty, or doubt. Instead, the faker blusters, covers up, stumbles, doubles down on error, and falls facedown. Fakers think that asking questions is for losers and shows weakness. But faking it invites exposure as a liar. It is far better to be exposed for honest mistakes and gaps in knowledge than for pulling a fast one.

So, what does humility in action look like? I might summarize it as a balance between authority, camaraderie, and receptivity. For example, after losing a big sales pitch, on a deal we should have won, I sat down with my team, not to point a finger but to learn how to be better. I went around the table to ask everyone how we could improve and grow. *Where did we miss a step? Where can we improve? How can we come together on this? How can I help us win next time? What do you need from me? What additional resources do you need?* You get the idea.

The faker CEO completely avoids the relevant issues, denies the problem, and blames others. *Get a different guy to sell the product.* Or: *Fire that guy.* Or: *Send out more emails slamming the competition.* Or: *Offer a discount.* For such CEOs, the fake it mindset is also short term and tactical. They end up seeing only what is down the hood, whereas reality-based leaders never lose sight of what is down the road. The trouble with being myopically transactional is that a business is supposed to survive beyond any one transaction. Longevity requires good distance vision, as I will discuss in chapter 6.

Give yourself time. Authentic, reality-based, values-based leadership requires building. And knowing is doing.

ONE TEAM, ONE DREAM

A critical piece of being an effective leader on the job is building the right leadership team around yourself. The best teams of any kind are those whose members possess skills that complement yours and each other's. Your team should broaden your perspective and your capacity to act. It should not simply duplicate you. If everyone is thinking the same way, nobody is thinking.

Whatever skills or expertise you need in your hires, focus on *qualities* that embody integrity and a respect for reality. Hire authenticity so that you will have at least as many reasons to avoid faking it as you have employees. It is a given, of course, that you want employees who are grounded, motivated, and good-natured. You need to staff for certain skill sets and expertise. But these requirements should not be allowed to override key aspects of personality and values.

In my career, I definitely made some bad hires. Some were really, *really* bad. The wrong hires were usually made when I:

- neglected to ask other people in my company to interview the candidate;
- really liked the candidate personally and hoped the individual would grow into a position; or
- was under time pressure and hired the first person I could recruit at that pressing moment.

By the way, harsh as this sounds, the sooner you face reality and get rid of your bad choices—people who are toxic—the better. One bad apple really can spoil the whole fruit bowl, and rapidly.

Conversely, the best people I hired were those who proved that they:

- could do things I could not;
- were self-motivated self-starters with energy and ideas;
- respected me and my authority;
- respected others;
- respected themselves;
- would tell me what I needed to hear, not what I wanted to hear;
- had passion and were clearly excited by and engaged with my vision and plan;
- saw working in my organization as a career opportunity; and
- were grounded in and fully identified with my core values, which were also those of the company.

THROUGH THICK AND THIN

If I had to characterize my experience as a CEO over the twenty-four-year life span of my company, I would put it into two big buckets labeled "Fun" and "Really Hard." Andy Grove, founder of Intel and author of *Only the Paranoid Survive*, had two better terms: "peacetime" and "wartime." The difference between the two is mostly a function of what is happening *to* your company due to external factors. Let me tell you, it was very hard to be a competent leader in both scenarios. They are at complete opposite ends of the spectrum, requiring entirely different management *approaches*, as well as different *teams* to augment your skill set.

In the first ten years, it was all about building and growing during the rise of enterprise software and the Internet—a time of incredible, seemingly endless opportunity. We brought home the bacon, fried it up in the pan, and lots of it. This was peacetime: creating culture, thinking big picture, and exploring new ideas for the joy of it. In addition to my initial crew, I hired leaders who wanted to build and who were entrepreneurial themselves. They were fundamental in establishing our US geographic expansion strategy and global reach, building our infrastructure and the foundation for our service offering.

The second ten years or so was wartime. It was more about fighting for and protecting our growth through economic downturns, rapid tech cycle turnover, the evolution of the PR industry, and unforeseen crises. It was about finding and fighting for the wins and focusing on the must-haves over the nice-to-haves. Here, I needed leaders capable of quickly pivoting from selling in a growth market to scraping it together in a contracting one. They were relentless and tough, and together we made lemonade out of some pretty rotten lemons.

Finally, during the last few years, I needed leaders who would help me stabilize and run a tight ship, preparing the business for acquisition. You want to keep innovating while also fighting to defend your innovations and optimizing every aspect of your business to be highly profitable.

Bottom line: Filling your leadership team with people who have the skills and the stamina to be successful in both good and in not-so-good times is just as important as hiring people who embody your values, are passionate, and so on. As much as possible, you need to hire for where you think your business is headed, not just where you are today. And that takes a keen awareness of your own strengths and weaknesses, and of what is going on in your market and in the rest of the economy.

THE WHOLE THING ABOUT BEING A WOMAN

I am ending this chapter about becoming a CEO with the topic of gender. Maybe you are wondering why this hasn't come up sooner, though it should be clear by now that this book is for everyone interested in leadership and business success, regardless of gender. Nonetheless, I am a woman, and that makes me more interesting. Quite frankly, I was probably a novelty in 1991, as a twenty-nine-year-old woman building my own business in the male-dominated tech industry. Gender, like race, is part of who we are, and to deny any part of ourselves is to deny reality.

Although I believe gender should be regarded as irrelevant to leadership, the reality is that it most certainly is an element of personality and therefore is a factor in leadership. As a result, becoming a CEO does call for putting gender into perspective. This begins by understanding that effective leadership is not about being either a man or a woman but about being smart, doing your homework, and staying true to yourself while applying that truth to the enterprise.

Of course I was conscious of the fact that I am a woman, but whenever I was in a business setting, meeting, or discussion, I never really thought about it. My gender was irrelevant to the matter at hand, at least to me, so I never felt the need to prepare for it, to compensate for it, or to play into it. I was just a person with something important to say, a vessel containing valuable knowledge. Maybe people expected me, as a young woman, to be more demure or unsure of myself. It never occurred to me to validate such expectations by faking a demeanor that just wasn't me. I think my employees respected and needed that from me, too.

I did not wonder what was going through a sixty-year-old man's mind while he was talking to this woman half his age who was operating a PR start-up. Honestly, I didn't have time to even think about it. I was too busy making certain I was always super prepared, wicked sharp, and bringing ideas and strategies to the table. I earned others' respect by being this way. If I ever failed to come across in a given pitch or engagement, it was because I had somehow failed to be sufficiently thorough or creative, or hadn't done enough research, or had done the wrong research, or had brought the wrong people to the meeting. In my mind, at least, it was never because I was a young female.

In my career, I met only a handful of men who dismissed me or did not want to do business with me because I am a woman. I found these men to be narrow-minded and weak, so I had no patience for them. In any case, they would have been terrible clients. Instead, I found plenty more people who *did* want to do business with me and for whom my gender never mattered.

DEALING WITH GENDER BIAS

All that being said, let me be clear here. Just because my gender did not loom large in my own consciousness does not mean I never had to deal with gender bias. I decided to build my own company and to make that company a place in which I wanted to work. I was intensely curious to see if I could be successful on my own terms. As CEO, I naturally had a measure of choice in the people with whom I chose to work and do business, but I still encountered plenty of gender bias, either directed at me in person or, indirectly, through my employees. Even if you are running the operation, you cannot simply erase centuries of gender-focused behavior. That bias is real, and it is everywhere.

What you *can* do is tune your own actions, including how you react to men who behave badly, who don't want to pay your invoices because they think they can bully you, who say disrespectful things about you to others in the industry, and who engage in other unacceptable behaviors. There are ways of dealing with men (and, I'm sorry to say, some women) who act like that.

Take Steve, a vice president of marketing, who demanded that I meet him for lunch to discuss his dissatisfaction with our work. For him, apparently, "discussion" required that I repeatedly feel his hand on my upper thigh—until I ordered a hot cup of coffee with dessert and tipped it onto his lap. Steve, by the way, never asked me out to lunch again, but the complaints vaporized.

Or there was Al, a chief marketing officer who, in addition to flirting with a female member of my team, also wanted to make his budget look better by "forgetting" to pay us for three months, until I spoke with a board member I made it my business to know. I relayed the details, and in the course of further diligence, other poor behavior on Al's part was discovered. In consequence, he was dismissed.

Or Roxanne. She was the new CEO of a high-paying, long-standing client who made it a habit to verbally abuse the men on my team until, on my way to the airport one day, I called her, fired her as my client, and told her that no one ever gets to treat my people that way.

I could go on—and, unfortunately, on. You could make a movie out of all the insulting incidents I saw and dealt with. I think, over time, I developed something of a reputation for pushing back on that BS. Being authentic and true to your values demands that you stand up for yourself, your company, and your employees, even if this risks alienating a client or deliberately jettisoning one. Your company will be stronger for it, even if it means losing that revenue. No deal is fair and no revenue source is clean if hanging on to it compromises your values.

In fact, if you fail to take a stand, you become complicit in others' bad behavior, making you, in essence, fake what you stand for. There is a price to pay for that, when your head hits the pillow at night, in how your employees will perceive you, and in the precedent you set that this sort of behavior is somehow acceptable, which it surely is not.

Values express, as well as build, character, and character is destiny. As a CEO, I have always sought to shape my own attitude, mindset, and character to control my destiny. Whether in the context of gender or of any other dimension of business, life, or business life, controlling your destiny is the hallmark of reality-based leadership. As such, it is the ultimate act of authenticity, which, as we will see in chapter 4, is essential to creating and presenting your company as what savvy marketers most highly value: an authentic brand.

CHAPTER FOUR

BECOMING AND STAYING AN AUTHENTIC BRAND

There is a plethora of excellent books about branding and brand management, and I am not going to try to boil that ocean here. Instead, this chapter focuses on how the values of the reality-based leader permeate a corporate culture and are critical to the creation and long-term success of an organization's brand.

There are many definitions of "brand." I think of it simply as the unique relationship a person has with a company and what the company produces and sells. Successful brands create the feeling of trust that buying a certain company's products or services delivers real and reliable benefits. To succeed, a brand must always represent reality. It must be and remain authentic. Yet, as we know, reality is always changing. Businesses grow, markets shift, and buying behaviors evolve. Creating an authentic brand is hard enough. Evolving and maintaining that brand's authenticity over time is extraordinarily complex and challenging, both art and science.

But at the core, there is also something starkly simple about it. A brand's representation of reality begins with and grows under the leadership of a company's founders, its CEO, and its top executives. It continually surprises me that so many leaders fail to grasp how much the creation and protection of a sustainable brand is in their hands. Too often, they think that branding is something that comes "later." Assigned to consultants and marketing people with varying degrees of expertise, the creation of the brand is put at risk of becoming a kind of bolt-on feature. That doesn't mean it's fake; it's just not very organic to the product, the service, or the organization. This can diminish its authenticity. A brand should be rooted in a company's heritage and culture, connected to a set of core values that are the company's very reason for being.

THE VALUE OF LEADERSHIP

A reality-grounded CEO manages, protects, and leads the brand by managing, protecting, and leading the culture and values behind it.

A 2019 trend report from Forrester Research predicted in 2020 that consumers would search for "deeper meaning" in the products and services they purchase, going on to explain, "More than 55% of consumers will consider company values when making a buying decision."[1] Companies that do succeed will cocreate values-driven experiences with customers and employees.

The 2019 report came out before the COVID-19 pandemic, which has made its insights even more important. For the next several years, I believe love-based marketing and empathetic, values-based communication, something about which I have spoken and written,[2] will play an increasingly important role in branding. Going forward, it will be about connecting with consumers and the consumer experience on a much deeper level, to win their trust and make them feel safe. Successful brands will need to exude messages of care and understanding (as opposed to fear), of hope for a better tomorrow, and to inspire their audiences with courage, resilience, and inclusivity.

For many leaders, this will require revisiting and perhaps reprioritizing their core values in the context of the current environment. It also will require a serious shift in marketing strategy to address what a July 2020 article from research firm Gartner Group calls a wave of "systemic mistrust," in which consumer trust has reached new lows. It is "possible that over the long term," Gartner observed, "a common enemy in the virus will inspire empathy, common purpose and cooperation, which will benefit brands that broadcast messages of openness, authenticity, and empathy."[3]

Furthermore, we know from research issued by Weber Shandwick, a global public relations firm, that global executives attribute 45% of their company's reputation and 44% of their company's market value to the reputation of their CEO. This is the so-called CEO reputation premium, and in addition to enhancing market value, a strong CEO reputation is overwhelmingly important in attracting investors, generating positive media attention, affording crisis protection, attracting new employees, and retaining current employees.[4]

Recall what happened when Steve Jobs, so thoroughly identified with the value of Apple, passed away in 2011. Speculation was rampant that the Apple brand of quality, must-have design, service, and innovation would slump. But while Jobs was a creative genius and a celebrity, his public reputation was often described as hot-tempered, mercurial, and tyrannical. The new CEO, Tim Cook, formerly Apple's chief operating officer, was largely unknown by comparison and lacked Jobs's larger-than-life presence. Consumers and investors alike wondered, with Jobs gone, would Apple's magic go along with him? Would even the Apple loyalists stray and key talent jump ship?

Cook was his own man and neither evaded nor denied these concerns. He was no Steve Jobs and he did not try to be. Knowing full well that consumers and investors were watching, Cook authentically and meticulously proved that, despite the changing of the guard, every feature of the brand and of the company's financial performance would remain consistent. By 2020, in fact, he had led Apple to become the first American company to achieve a trillion-dollar valuation. Under his leadership, the brand continued to fulfill its promise with subsequent releases of the iPhone, Apple Watch, AirPods, and other devices. Cook also took on social causes such as the environment and diversity, something for which Jobs didn't have much of an appetite. Of course, it was the people of Apple who carried this out, but the commitment to the brand flowed from him. All in all, it was a remarkably successful evolution of leadership, values, and brand.

Not all CEOs are brands in themselves, and few CEOs are seamlessly identified with their companies and brands. Most aren't. In fact, many of the brands with which we identify are simply product names, like Oreo, PAM, SlimFast, Varathane, and WD-40. We may have no sense of the people or companies behind them.

Whatever your branding strategy, however, it is always based on a belief and value system that was created by someone—an inventor, founder, entrepreneur, or leader—who stands behind it. At the end of the day, it is the leadership of a company, the CEO, who is responsible for the success and failure of their business and the brands they represent.

TO PRODUCE A HIGH-VALUE BRAND, CREATE A HIGH-VALUE CULTURE

At the beginning of this book, I mentioned how critical it is for a founder to establish the initial core values of her company. These are articulated in a values statement: a list of your core beliefs and values; what you and your company stand for (not who you wish you could become). They don't have to be elaborate or grandiose. When I started my company (and it was literally just me, myself, and I), my values fit on an index card—with space to spare:

Be smart
Deliver results
Be honest
Be grateful
Move fast

Brief as they were, these were the foundation of our culture and brand. As a company grows, your initial values expand and infuse the policies and processes you establish. You must think about how they will permeate every aspect of your business, in product development and testing, customer service, employee performance programs and benefits, marketing campaigns, financial reporting, internal communication, and competitive positioning. Furthermore, your culture is based on how you and your leadership team act and behave—where you take your team out for drinks, how you manage through a crisis, the quality of the people in your network, even your office decor. You model the values that create a culture.

I remember when I was interviewing the head of engineering at a network management software start-up that had just become our client. We were talking about the company's culture and values in preparation for a press launch.

"We don't have a culture. We just work hard," he said, and then he proceeded to tell me in hushed tones that he was interviewing at other companies.

Ugh. He had just spoken volumes about his firm's leadership and future viability.

A strong culture will keep you and your employees from faking it. And it will be instrumental in building a strong brand for your company. All of this—and it is a lot—should be set up early, as you are building and growing your business. You must communicate the values and your desired culture in words, directly, and you have to make it clear that you and everyone else in the organization must honor and protect that culture.

Our values statement (after we actually *became* a company and had more than a handful of employees) stayed in place for about ten years or so. It was quite lengthy in its detail, so I've condensed it here.

TEAMWORK We pledge to be supportive and accountable, to share responsibilities, to believe in ourselves, and to work together as a family and in teams to support our clients.

EDUCATION We strive to be the best at our jobs by continuously learning new skills, growing in our strategic expertise and proficiency, our well-roundedness, and our mastery of our job responsibilities.

ACCOUNTABILITY We promise to our clients and to each other to be trustworthy, reliable, productive, and dependable, to follow through, and to produce high-quality, error-free work.

MOTIVATION We are always resourceful, never cookie cutter. We have a can-do, energetic attitude, go the extra mile, and are always proactive in the work we do for our clients.

HUMOR We work hard and play hard, and our glass is always half full. We find opportunities to laugh and always find a way to make things work.

INTEGRITY Integrity is a combination of humility, honesty, ethics, morals, accuracy, and precision. We take pride in our work and we give it, and everything we say and do, our honest and best attention. We admit mistakes and uphold the company's values and standards.

These values were tweaked over the years, until I later revised and modernized them, with much input from our employees and clients. The following statement covered roughly the second half of my company's life. Again, each value was followed by a lot of detail about what it meant in practice. It was important that it all tied together.

WE'RE A FAMILY We have each other's backs and we care about each other.

WE'RE DRIVEN We succeed based on our own merit and entrepreneurial spirit.

WE ARE BOLD We think on our feet and are never afraid to try something new.

WE ARE INVESTED We produce results that move our clients' businesses forward.

INTEGRITY ABOVE ALL We do the right thing, in the right way.

WE NEVER GIVE UP Period.

It is interesting to compare this second list to the first. In some ways, it is more mature and clear, and in other ways it is rather similar, including the use of identical words and themes: family, creativity, integrity, results, success, and persistence. In communicating these values at our all-hands meeting one day, I expressed their importance.

"Values are the reason people come here, why they stay, and why they come back," I said. "They are the reason we've been in business for this long. These are not one-word posters with sunsets, seagulls, and rainbows in the background. They are from the heart and they are the bones of this company. They give us something to hold us to, strive for, and are something to be proud of and commended for."

A values statement defines priorities, business practices, and standards. It defines who you are and identifies to whom you are beholden. Stating your priorities, in turn, leads you in creating the tactics to accomplish your strategic objectives. Your culture and business practices emanate from your values, and your brand, in turn, reflects them. They are like a crown (figure 2). You can see how values, culture, and practices drive up through an organization to create its brand and, if you will, its accompanying halo effect.

VALUES, CULTURE, AND BRAND IN HARMONY

Let me offer a specific example. One of the core values of my firm was to be results-driven and thoroughly invested in our clients. That meant exceeding clients' expectations of our service. Stating our core values informed and guided what we needed to *do* as a company and prompted some of these tactical actions.

- **Internal troubleshooting sessions.** To anticipate issues before they turned into problems, we convened monthly troubleshooting meetings with account team and nonteam members. At first, employees resisted these meetings, feeling defensive about their work. Acceptance came when managers proved it was okay to talk about problems without fearing blowback and when staff acknowledged that every account had problems that needed solving. Another positive side effect came in the identification of new ideas that could potentially deliver additional results to our clients.

- **External big picture discussions.** While the troubleshooting meetings focused on short- to midterm issues, higher-level conversations with our clients' CEOs, execs, and board members took us out of the day-to-day, gave us new ideas, and brought a longer-term, more strategic dimension to our work. These meetings involved the most senior members of my company (including me) and were wide-ranging, covering topics from future product development to competitive concerns, upcoming expansion, and partnerships.

■ **Unexpected value-added services.** We offered multidimensional programs, with services outside of our immediate purview, such as events management, Web application development, and introductions to venture capitalists for outside funding. These capabilities and relationships were out of the realm of the typical engagement. They offered clients value that felt like bonuses to their contracts, even as they helped drive results.

FIGURE 2   Values, Culture, and Brand

- **The "whole" customer.** We took a broad, 360-degree view of every client engagement, from how we connected with our clients' receptionist to relationships we forged with board members, investors, sales staff, engineers, and, of course, their marketing people. These different perspectives colored our programs, enhanced our knowledge, infused our story-telling with new angles, and deepened relationships. Specific agency personnel were assigned to specific client personnel based on role and chemistry.

- **Client feedback.** I gave strong consideration to client satisfaction in employee performance reviews. This input was largely derived from quarterly conversations my partners and I had with our clients, aimed at learning what was working on their accounts, where there was room for improvement, and who they felt were our star performers. (For a while, we issued online surveys to our clients, but the personal conversations produced far more valuable feedback and clients greatly appreciated the attention.)

- **Employee recognition.** We were never stingy with employee recognition for exceptional client results, which was shared at our all-hands company meetings. We created a "wall of fame" to showcase the most excellent and meaningful results our employees generated.

- **It's the how, not the what.** We showed our clients *how* we would support them. Sharing with them our methodology became as valuable as telling them *what* we would do for them. This set us apart from other firms our size (as I will discuss further in chapter 8).

You can see how articulating a specific value focused on delivering exceptional client service infused our processes and culture. It touched how we behaved and talked to one another internally as well as how we presented ourselves to prospects and developed relationships with the press, how we carried ourselves at networking events, and (this is important but often overlooked) how we spoke about work to our family and friends. Not every client was delighted with our work, and we definitely weren't always perfect, but we did earn a reputation as a quality shop with high standards that consistently delivered results and cared deeply about providing client value. Had we failed to establish and inculcate that value, I'm certain we would not have unilaterally aimed as high or tried as hard, which in the end would have produced only average results and an equivalent reputation.

Another key value and aspect of our culture was the notion of "family" and "team," which was centered around employee development and retention. In the early 1990s, a lot of agencies were known as "body shops," demanding work for long hours at subpar pay in the interest of generating big profits that most employees never got to enjoy. The average retention rate of a midlevel person in the tech PR agency world was eighteen months. It's hard to grow a business and provide quality client service when you're constantly turning over your staff.

From the outset, my goal was to create a culture in which I wanted to work. I craved a culture that would motivate employees to stay with my company, to learn, and to build their careers over time while growing our organization. I believed that if my employees were happy, they would give that extra 5% to make our clients happy. Continuity of staff meant continuity of business. Everything began and ended with my employees.

This devotion manifested itself in vigorous employee professional development programs with internal brown bag sessions, outside speakers, management training, a focus on mentoring, and a budget for each employee to attend the seminars and networking events that interested them. We also led the industry with benefits, including one of the industry's first work-from-home programs, our Creative Working Solution policy for new mothers, highly competitive salaries, extensive vacation and health insurance policies, cool office space, an incentive quarterly bonus program, a 401(k) with a company match, and a trust fund with a $1,000 contribution that we set up on behalf of each child born to a company employee. All of these were impressive at the time, and pretty spectacular for a firm of our size.

While our benefits were great, what mattered most was a working environment in which people knew they could be themselves, where everyone's voice and opinion mattered, and where ideas were valued, heard, and considered. It was an environment that encouraged creativity and an entrepreneurial spirit, which I fostered by being open to new business ideas from our employees.

Case in point: One of our earliest employees, Mike Teeling, believed we needed to be more adept at coaching and preparing our clients for the press meetings and presentations we arranged. He developed from scratch a new service he called VoicePower, and he wrote and presented the business plan to the leadership team. He convinced us of its validity and taught me and others how to deliver it. Over time, this service grew, and it added tremendous value for our clients and revenue to our bottom line. VoicePower is still in existence today, almost thirty years later, at Finn Partners, the firm that bought my company.

Of course, not every idea was implemented, but any idea that made good business sense was heard and entertained.

Finally, and very importantly, we also had a "no assholes" policy. This applied to both clients and employees. We did not tolerate bad behavior or office politics, and those who played that game never lasted long.

PRIDE, PASSION, AND RESULTS

To be clear, I certainly didn't have this all ironed out the day we won our first client, or even when we incorporated. The tactics, processes, and programs were created over time, with the help of several others. I didn't fully realize just how much these values would shape our brand. What I did know from the beginning was what mattered to *me*, and what I wanted *my* company to stand for. I made it a point to discuss our values and culture regularly at our monthly leadership team meetings, and I continually consulted with others, especially our employees, about what was important to them.

In the end, our culture, with its values focused on employees and client service, represented a lot of the goodness of our brand. For a long time, we had a framed poster in our lobby that simply said, "Pride, Passion, and Results." I didn't wake up one morning and impose these words on our employees; they just naturally evolved out of years of our camaraderie, work, and spirit. I guess you could say it was the culmination of all our values, our culture, and our brand, summed up in those three magic words. It became our mantra, an internal tagline of sorts.

Our values and culture served us well, resulting in better employee retention and industry awards both for great client campaigns and for being a good place to work. It produced a halo effect that helped make our firm one of the most enduring agency brands in the tech industry. Of course, we had to uphold that standard over the long haul or it wouldn't have stuck.

This was at times extremely difficult.

Laying off people in your "family" due to business declines during an economic downturn flies in the face of a culture committed to employee retention. There were, admittedly, also periods when we lost sight of these values, when we were distracted by other business initiatives or consumed by a need to bring in revenue. But we always strove to come back to those values and to give them new meaning. During those times, I tried to be transparent with my employees about how and why we had strayed and about how we were going to move forward, perhaps differently, but once again in alignment with our values. I know that having those values and holding them high was a key to our authenticity and, therefore, to our longevity.

A BIT ABOUT MISSION STATEMENTS

As values inform culture and brand, they also should inform other important foundational company messages, such as the mission statement. Unfortunately, most mission statements (and for that matter, vision statements) are utterly bland and soulless. They are the ultimate expression of fakery when they aren't authentic. In fact, you're probably better off without one if it reads like something any other company could say.

How do you avoid the pitfall of a vapid, phony mission statement? It has to flow from the current state of your business and define the overall purpose of your company relative to your customers' needs and your company's values. (By contrast, a vision statement is an inspirational, future-oriented statement of where you want your company to *be*, and how you intend to effect change relative to the future of your industry or society.) Most important, it has to sound like something you, its leader, would actually say (and mean it).

Here was ours at one point: "Our mission is to be the best independent US tech PR firm that delivers the most innovative and impactful digital communications to help B2B tech companies become market leaders." (Our vision statement was "To help achieve economic and social progress by making the disruptive changes created by technology understandable, acceptable and embraceable with clear, truthful and compelling communications.")

These statements suited us at the time. At the other end of the spectrum, here is the mother of all corporate mission statements, Johnson & Johnson's "Credo," created by Robert Wood Johnson, the company's founder, in 1943. It is kind of a value, mission, and vision statement all rolled into one, and it is still prominent on the company's website today.

> We believe our first responsibility is to the patients, doctors and nurses, to mothers and fathers and

all others who use our products and services. In meeting their needs everything we do must be of high quality. We must constantly strive to provide value, reduce our costs and maintain reasonable prices. Customers' orders must be serviced promptly and accurately. Our business partners must have an opportunity to make a fair profit.

We are responsible to our employees who work with us throughout the world. We must provide an inclusive work environment where each person must be considered as an individual. We must respect their diversity and dignity and recognize their merit. They must have a sense of security, fulfillment and purpose in their jobs. Compensation must be fair and adequate and working conditions clean, orderly and safe. We must support the health and well-being of our employees and help them fulfill their family and other personal responsibilities. Employees must feel free to make suggestions and complaints. There must be equal opportunity for employment, development and advancement for those qualified. We must provide highly capable leaders and their actions must be just and ethical.

We are responsible to the communities in which we live and work and to the world community as well. We must help people be healthier by supporting better access and care in more places around the world. We must be good citizens—support good works and charities, better health and education, and bear our fair share of taxes. We must maintain in good order the property we are privileged to use, protecting the environment and natural resources.

Our final responsibility is to our stockholders.
Business must make a sound profit. We must exper-
iment with new ideas. Research must be carried on,
innovative programs developed, investments made
for the future and mistakes paid for. New equipment
must be purchased, new facilities provided, and new
products launched. Reserves must be created to provide for adverse times. When we operate according
to these principles, the stockholders should realize a
fair return.[5]

Whether you are the leader of a start-up, a Fortune 100 corporation, or an entity somewhere in between, you can see how
central, and uniquely personal, the establishment of one's core
values are to shaping a company's culture and business practices,
an enduring brand, and yes, an authentic mission statement.
Of course, there are many other components you should build
out as part of determining your company's value proposition,
market, product and competitive positioning, differentiation,
and so forth. They are all part of developing your brand and can
require considerable investment of time and resources. Bottom
line, though: they all begin and end with what you stand for.

ENDURING BRANDS

Think about other enduring value-based brands. They stood
the test of time because they remained authentic, evolving with
the times while staying true to themselves. They were not built
on spin but are connected with real values that are pervasive in
their corporate cultures and messaging.

Look at Budweiser. Why is it America's most successful beer
brand? Bud may not be the best *beer*, but its long-term success
makes it arguably one of the best beer *brands*.

Why?

The company creates values, and it markets consistently with them. For instance, its ads are culturally relevant to its customer base. Its 2016 Super Bowl ad was all about the company founder, Adolphus Busch, who immigrated to the United States to "pursue his dream of brewing the 'King of Beers.'" The ad celebrated diversity and linked its founder's dream to the American dream. These are solid, sympathetic values. Budweiser also sponsors the sports teams, music events, and festivals its customers love.[6]

Or consider Prologis, a company in logistics real estate, run by chairman and CEO Hamid R. Moghadam. Prologis, which is on the Corporate Knights Global 100 Most Sustainable Corporations in the World list, is the first logistics real estate company to issue green bonds, and it is deeply committed to environmental stewardship, social responsibility, and corporate governance. Its values of growth, productivity, and resilience create value for customers, investors, and communities and support the environment, which in turn helps it to grow its business—it had $148 billion assets under management in 2020, up from $118.4 billion in 2019.[7]

In 1991, corporate values, culture, and belief systems were a novel concept in the tech industry, yet they were incredibly important to PeopleSoft founder Dave Duffield. Over time, the company adhered to and adapted those values even while experiencing high growth, bringing a new technology to market, and undertaking an initial public offering. The company's executives were always grounded in a powerfully customer-focused vision, which most certainly contributed to its success as a business and to its incredible brand.

Let's not neglect the many millions of family-owned businesses and smaller companies passed on from generation to generation. They made it because they never faked what they stood for. Take P. C. Richard & Son, one of the largest chains of private, family-owned appliance, television, electronics, and

mattress stores in the United States. It was founded in 1909 by
Pieter Christian Richard as a small hardware store called Work
Well Done, in Brooklyn, New York. Talk about putting your
money where your mouth is! Its core values and mission were
the actual name of the business. Now in its fifth generation of
family management and an estimated $1 billion in revenue, it's
not so small anymore.

Or take Louie's, the diner right by the train station in
Manhasset, New York. A family institution since 1963, they can
always be counted on to open early for the Wall Street crowd
and to serve your eggs just the way you want them. Or Buck's of
Woodside, California, founded by Jamis MacNiven in 1991. It
gained fame as a breakfast spot for venture capitalists and tech
entrepreneurs in Silicon Valley. Now run by MacNiven's sons and
entering its thirtieth year, Buck's still serves the best pancakes west
of the Mississippi.

Sure, the employees at both of those establishments got new
aprons, some new items were added to the menus, and the seats
have been reupholstered since their founding. But their core
values never really changed, nor did their love for the community, their food, and how it made people feel. Had they strayed
too far from their values, tried to modernize too much, and
altered their brand, they would have become something they
weren't, and perhaps lost their following.

The point in these examples is that all those critical elements
of values, culture, and brand stayed in authentic harmony
through time.

COMMODITIZATION IS A BRAND, TOO

Let's take a deep breath here and recognize that a lot of companies
never get around to articulating their values, and yet they nevertheless achieve success. The reality is that there are companies
that don't care much about culture and, furthermore, don't need
to create a big brand for their particular type of business. Many

of the employees—and even executives—at such companies just want to work somewhere that pays well and offers good benefits. *Love your job?* they scoff. *Love your family. Or just get a dog.*

Bottom line: You have to do what is right for your business and for you, and there is a time, need, and place when running or being employed by a company like this makes perfectly good sense (as long as it is ethical, of course). But for companies in industries where brand awareness matters (consumer product goods, health care, food and beverage, automotive, technology, and others), and for people who derive meaning from being associated with them, indifference can lead to loss of market position, or worse.

Companies that do not articulate a values-driven vision can run the risk of slipping into commoditization. That is, without such an inspiring vision, it becomes more difficult to create a brand that has a strong personality and a lasting relationship with its customers. Without such a brand, all you have left are commodities, which consumers choose or don't choose based simply on price and availability. It is the difference between Coca-Cola and cola.

For employees and managers without a values-driven vision, inspiration becomes elusive or simply irrelevant. This contributes to commoditization of everything the firm produces—and even worse, it commoditizes the company's personnel as well. Nevertheless, in many industries and many markets, commodity goods and services do well enough to put bread on the table and new tires on the car.

FALLING FROM GRACE

Of course, it is also true that having a good brand does not automatically save you from faltering. Brands and the companies behind them can fall prey to two broad categories of danger. They can fail to evolve appropriately and competitively, or they can suffer serious compromise. Let's look at the latter first.

The warning signs in a shift of values are policies and processes that are being overlooked, ignored, or purposely violated. Give such lapses a pass and the whole organization can become corrupt in a way that will erode and ultimately destroy its brand. The leadership team of a company must be capable of recognizing such a slide and have the power to blow the whistle and correct the course. On the other hand, some leaders intentionally deceive their customers and are, or become, morally corrupt. The old proverb that a fish stinks from the head down is true; for better or worse, culture and brand come from the top.

Let's take Uber. Its cofounder and former CEO, Travis Kalanick, was engulfed in sexual harassment allegations and was the subject of a video showing him berating Uber drivers. At the time, entire communities banned Uber because of the company's terrible reputation for exploiting gig workers and promoting an abusive culture.[8] Even with a new CEO, new policies, and improved governance, that stigma still hangs like a cloud over the company today.

Or consider Volkswagen. The company was born with the worst possible leadership heritage—it was a pet project of Adolf Hitler. The "people's car" company survived World War II, rehabilitated itself by engaging the counterculture values of the 1960s, and made the classic and iconic VW Beetle. In the spirit of environmental responsibility, VW produced a diesel line with high efficiency, decent acceleration, and incredibly low emissions numbers.

In September 2015, however, the Environmental Protection Agency discovered that many VW diesel cars sold in the United States had software that was deliberately designed to defeat emissions testing. In fact, the VW diesel engines produced levels of emissions that were too high to meet EPA standards. Maybe the software was installed to buy time to create a genuine low-emission system, or maybe VW never intended to do the necessary engineering. Either way, VW faked it big-time. The EPA ordered a massive recall, VW's stock fell 37%, CEO Martin Winterkorn resigned (and was charged with fraud and conspiracy), and the company pleaded guilty, paying $4.3 billion in fines.[9]

And let's not forget Theranos. It was marketed to investors largely on the strength of its values. Founder and CEO Elizabeth Holmes promised to democratize health care by making blood-based testing easy, painless, and cheap. As it turned out, the connection between the values Holmes articulated and the reality her company created was utterly fake.

Most examples of brands that have damaged their authenticity do not involve criminal fraud or even straying from their core values. Carelessness and complacency are often the culprit.

When Coca-Cola, usually meticulous about protecting its brand, first began marketing in China, it was shocked to find that its name translated to "Bite the Wax Tadpole" or "Female Horse Stuffed with Wax," depending on the dialect. The Puffs toilet tissue brand did not bother to research the German language until after it discovered that *Puff* is slang for "porn." Too late. The product was on German shelves. Both Coke and Puffs were lazy and cut valuable corners in their global marketing research. The point is that you cannot cut *any* corners when it comes to the value of your brand.[10]

Respecting your brand's values also means devoting great care to the products you produce—and release. In the 1980s, R. J. Reynolds rushed to market the Premier, the first smokeless cigarette, even though testers said it smelled like horse manure. And who can forget Samsung's Galaxy Note 7, its flagship smartphone of 2016, which was equipped with faulty lithium ion batteries that sometimes caught fire or exploded? Cutting corners in manufacturing and quality are unacceptable for a trusted brand.[11]

Finally, there are examples of brands that became overly confident and somehow lost touch with their authenticity—like when *Cosmopolitan* magazine decided to get into the yogurt business or when Harley-Davidson decided to "make" aftershave, perfume, and wine coolers. This was just too much of a departure from either company's brand promise. They were both way over their skis in thinking that consumers would yearn to buy yogurt from a magazine publisher or perfume from a rugged motorcycle company. Customers just couldn't make that leap of faith. More to the point, they were offended.[12] Both *Cosmo* and Harley were faking it, trying to become something they were not and could never be. Ultimately, they listened to their disgruntled customers and retrenched.

PROTECT YOUR BRAND

The hardest thing about building a great brand is keeping it that way. What can leaders and executives do to stay grounded and protect brand authenticity? The easy part is to make sure you've done everything you can to protect your brand legally, including domains, copyrights, patents, and trademarks. The rest is more involved, and you have to be relentless about it.

- **Understand "efficiency cuts."** Avoid shortcuts that promise to reduce costs or that masquerade as "efficiency." Any shortcut that compromises thoroughness or quality erodes values, culture, and, inevitably, brand. Listen to what your people tell you, but make sure you are clear on the benefits and even clearer on the downsides to any proposed shortcut.

- **Investigate expansion and contraction initiatives.** Take the time and effort to really understand what's behind any proposed expansion into new geographies, product lines, or customer segments. Investigate why certain markets are being cut or why a product is being discontinued. Go back to your core values and beliefs. Does it fit the brand promise? Is there enough research to validate the move? Does everything still hold true? Question every incomplete or evasive answer.

Resist the urge to just press the Go button if something doesn't feel 100%.

- **Personally monitor employee morale.** See and be seen with your people. Go to the cafeteria and eat with them. Attend the family picnic. Talk to their spouses. Spend your time talking with people you never talk to. Ask them how it's going and what's not working. Tell them you'll look into it, and then get back to them. When those who work with or for you begin to feel dissatisfied, uneasy, queasy, or worse, you can be sure that something is brewing.

- **Listen to the voice of your customers.** Depending on your type of business, form a customer advisory council and offer customers savings on products for their input. Pay close attention to your online reputation. Get timely reports and study them. In large measure, customers speak with their wallets, but they speak with feedback, too. One way or another, they will tell you when you have disappointed them. If you hear this, don't argue. Instead, respond with genuine gratitude and address the problems, which may be rooted in brand values that are under attack.

- **Watch for subcultures.** As you grow, for example, creating a new division or acquiring another company, you need to accommodate and integrate other cultures. Finding new tools to encourage communication across groups, creating "champions" to interweave tasks between teams to foster connection, and putting an emphasis on inclusivity across the board are vital. Integration specialists can help you avoid disaster in the assimilation of new and differing behaviors, values, and, yes, brands.

- **Be different, not just better.** Look beyond your own company and study the competition. Know yourself and your company—relative to others, competitively. Being a competitive brand does not always mean being the better brand, which can be narrow thinking. Differentiating your brand is more about how you are different in terms of your value proposition. Sustaining relevant differentiation cuts through marketplace clutter and lives up to your brand every day.

Cultures, like brands, are living, breathing organisms. They are not a "set and forget" kind of thing. Core values can evolve, some moving up or down your list of priorities, fine-tuning and modernizing in definition or context, as was the case in my company's twenty-four-year history. Here, I was in lockstep with my partner, Shannon Latta. Among other things, Shannon ran the marketing of our company and looked after the evolution of our brand through a few gyrations of the US economy, the tech sector, and the PR industry. Part of staying an authentic brand is to undertake regular assessment of your values, culture, offering, positioning, and strategy in relation to the market and other external forces. The trick, once again, is to keep it from becoming stale while still being authentic, fresh, and harmonious—based, naturally, on reality.

NEVER DENY THE REALITY OF CHANGE

Unfortunately, not all CEOs or their top executives recognize brand erosion when they see it. They may be just too close to the business or distracted by other big initiatives. Perhaps you are working for an executive who is too busy, or worse, has become complacent. *We've been doing it this way for so long, why change?* they say. *If it ain't broke, don't fix it.*

Some CEOs don't listen to what their marketing and brand executives are telling them about changing buying behaviors and friction in the market. Maybe you are one of those marketing execs banging your head against a wall. Or maybe a new chief executive has just joined your company and is running with their own ideas, changing elements of the brand without respecting the core values behind it.

I've encountered the entire grab bag of executives who have their blinders on when it comes to company values, culture, and brand authenticity.

Take Prakash, the CEO of a four-year-old big data software company. He came to us looking for better messaging and positioning, and he wanted to strengthen brand awareness. But he had never articulated his values or mission and could not put a label on his culture, except for "We make it happen." Essentially, he had no brand awareness to even *begin* to strengthen. His concept of brand building was coming up with a new tagline: "We Make Your Big Data Small."

Ugh.

Next, take Colleen, successful serial CEO of several hot start-ups. She was brought in by investors to help pivot an online travel experience company—a challenging task in an already crowded space. Instead of studying consumer trends, doing the research, and finding the right competitive differentiation, she just wanted to be "like Orbitz." Literally. She handed us an outdated PowerPoint deck she had somehow gotten from someone at Orbitz, which laid out everything—brand promise, value proposition, mission statement, messaging, even the logo color guide—and directed us to copy it so her company could just "be" it.

Really?

Then there was James, chief marketing officer of a cyber-security company. He changed his positioning and messaging every six months because his CEO was getting pressure from board members. Nothing they tried was sticking or resonating in the market, revenues were down, and new competitors were entering the sector. The brand became so confused that no one knew who the company was anymore. That's what happens when you impulsively change your positioning. Actually, the bigger problem was that the company was changing its messaging in the hope of solving a revenue problem. It just doesn't work that way.

Painting your Prius bright red won't make it run like a Ferrari. You can't fabricate a brand by copying someone else's, and you can't change your company by putting a new sign on the door. A brand takes original thought, development, nurturing, and authenticity before it can grow and help your enterprise.

Our work in each of these cases began with helping the execs see the light. They needed a reset. Doing it right—which is the only way to do it—has to be grounded in reality and the truth.

IT'S YOUR BRAND. OWN IT.

In the end, you as the CEO, and by extension your leadership team, must steward your brand. You can shape it, grow it, modify it, but you must never let go of its function as the messenger of your company's promise. As the CEO, the top dog, word from you is powerful and packs a lot of juice. When it comes to branding, you are the ultimate keeper of the flame. You cannot delegate that responsibility entirely. If you do, you'll surrender control of your company's identity.

In the end, this is a major responsibility. You are the head of state of your company, what it stands for and its brand. You will need the help and advice of others. You must listen very carefully to your leadership team and to other stakeholders. You may at times feel lost in a clamoring crowd, but you must know that, despite all the noise around you, you alone are in charge and responsible. Ultimately, it all really does rest with you.

And that feeling is both very awesome and, at times, quite lonely.

CHAPTER FIVE

GET USED TO LONELY

Being an entrepreneur or founder/CEO can be described as many things: exciting, exhilarating, rewarding, difficult, stressful, and challenging. "Lonely" is probably the last word that comes to mind, unless you've sat in the chair before. But leadership definitely can be isolating, which may surprise you and even whup you pretty good. It may be a cliché to say that it's lonely at the top, but this is a real feeling, and it affects all leaders to some extent, at some point, in good times and in bad.

As *Harvard Business Review*'s first CEO Snapshot Survey noted, "Often dismissed and rarely discussed, many CEOs are plagued by feelings of isolation once they take on the top job."[1] Those feelings come in many forms: anxiety, fear, loneliness, sadness, even depression. They must be anticipated and dealt with. Unattended, CEO loneliness can chip away at your confidence and affect your judgment and performance. If you begin doubting yourself, feeling like maybe you've lost your mojo or you're somehow not worthy of your success, the imposter syndrome can knock on your door.

Some people are more susceptible to this C-level loneliness than others, especially entrepreneurs and, as *HBR* observed, first-time CEOs. In a job that has no manual, many of the situations and accompanying emotions you face will be new, and you'll have to face them in real time. You won't always know how to react, and the newness of everything can be overwhelming. Female executives are also uniquely susceptible. Being a trailblazer and breaking the glass ceiling comes with its own very unique set of challenges and emotions, not least of which is loneliness.

During twenty-four years as a founder/CEO, the "lonely cloud" certainly came over me from time to time. I'm going to help you understand the loneliness that comes with being a leader and suggest how you can create effective means to cope, and even to strengthen your leadership.

RELATIONSHIP DYNAMICS

The positional power that comes with having a C-level title changes normal relationship dynamics, sometimes in unexpected and disturbing ways. This often starts at home. Close family and friends may not know how to deal with your elevated role and responsibilities. Raining on your parade, some may belittle your entrepreneurial adventure and you along with it. You start to feel like maybe you're just not going to share your day or your little successes, in essence withdrawing to avoid drawing attention to yourself.

At work, your title can change how you view people who are nice to you. Is the employee who just brought you your favorite coffee drink brown-nosing you or being genuine? Such gestures of kindness can easily be construed—or is it misconstrued?—as opportunism on the part of someone who wants to ingratiate himself with you. *What does he* really *want from me?* Antennas up, your inclination to trust is reduced and you start to feel isolated from your own people.

How you respond as a CEO is important. You don't want to be seen as playing favorites or as being played. You also don't want to be perceived as ungrateful or to walk around being suspicious all the time. It's crazy that such a simple thing can cause such real problems, but it's the truth. You have to develop a reputation for being a smart, authentic, *grateful*, and *approachable* leader who also has a finely tuned bullshit meter. Easier said than done, but it must be done.

When you are the boss, there is a built-in level of separation from your people (figure 3). As my company got bigger, my employees began organizing their own after-work gatherings. I wasn't always invited. It made me feel left out and a little paranoid. Had I done or said something offensive? Were they talking about me? I wanted them to feel comfortable enough that we could all

FIGURE 3   Lonely CEO

hang out together. But their actions were normal and healthy. If you're the boss, you cannot *truly* be "one of them." You can be friendly with your employees but you cannot be their friend, because, trust me, doing so will get messy and ultimately will undermine your leadership, which you'll see later in this book.

DECISIONS, DECISIONS

As I discussed in chapter 2, decision-making is at the heart of leadership. Everything unfolds, expands, contracts, rises, and sinks as a result of the decisions that you, and you alone, make.

Depending on the structure of your leadership team, you may have partners who vote with you on big decisions. Other times, a company may have two CEOs or two C-level executives who divide and conquer on specific decisions. Most often, though, there is only one CEO, one chief decision maker, and the proverbial buck stops with that person.

In figuring out what to decide, you solicit input from your team, advisors, board members, customers, and others. You do this until you don't, when *you* have to make the final call. Your team will—you hope—support you, but it is your name on that decision. It feels lonely because you must make the decision alone. It feels especially lonely when the consequences are painful, like when you decide to do a layoff.

Sending good people whom *you* hired back home to their families to explain that they lost their jobs because of what *you* decided is one of the most horrible things a CEO has to do. Knowing that these people feel worse than you and that they probably resent you (or worse) only intensifies your disappointment, guilt, and isolation. You will also find no shortage of naysayers and critics who disagree with your decision. All of this can wear you down.

Sometimes being a CEO is lonely because you can't explain all the reasons behind the decisions you make. You want to be transparent but you can't, whether for legal reasons or because you don't want the people who still have a job to think your ship is sinking and quit. You need to be at once empathetic and kind but also positive and strong. You have to provide a path forward, even when you might not be feeling so great yourself. You hold it together for everyone else while keeping your own thoughts locked inside.

That is Lonely with a capital *L*.

The killer is, you'll find no peer, no other CEO, down the hall to talk to. Being able to relate to other people is vital to mental health and well-being. You can talk with your leadership team or your number 2, but on some level, you have to be strong for them, too. And when 100% of your friends are also in your business network, you have to be careful. Friends or not, you don't want to show cracks in your armor. This kind of self-exposure can unintentionally blow back on you, like the time I was having lunch with a brand-new client and Bill, a close industry friend, stopped over at our table.

BILL: Hi, Sabrina. How's business these days? You were going through a pretty rough time a couple months ago with those cutbacks.

ME: Hi, Bill! Let me introduce you to our brand-new client here, Kevin. Business has definitely improved and we were able to manage through all of that. So, what's going on with your . . . [blah, blah, blah—basically, any topic that will make Bill talk about himself]?

This was a no-harm, no-foul exchange (although somewhat uncomfortable), but there's a little lesson there. If you find yourself confiding in a friend who also happens to be in your industry, always follow up with a progress report. The last impression you leave is that person's reality, and that's a loose end you might want to tie up.

WHEN IT'S RAINING SIDEWAYS

Stress, tension, and anxiety are natural side effects of the sheer volume of business problems, unpleasant surprises, and crises that a CEO encounters. These things just come with the job. Over time, though, the cumulative effect can be illness, depression, or both.

It was late summer 2008, the beginning of the Great Recession and the start of several years of tough sledding. I was ill-equipped for what was coming my way. I was entering "wartime CEO" mode.

First, I had to decide whether we should close down our prized Boston office. One of my earliest employees and business partners, Mara Stefan, had led our first geographic expansion there in 1996, and we had a very successful twelve-year run. By this point, though, Mara had moved on, and while we made a valiant effort, we struggled to install permanent new leadership. Furthermore, the enterprise software market in Boston was consolidating and our client base was shrinking. While it accounted for roughly 15% of the firm's total revenue—still a decent chunk of change—our office lease was also about to expire, so pulling out was worth considering. Signing a new multiyear, multimillion-dollar lease felt really risky. Yet leaving a market where we were so established also meant terminating or relocating our remaining employees and telling our clients. The news could leak out into the industry, casting doubt on our viability and hindering our ability to win business elsewhere.

In New York, our clients in the advertising technology (adtech) sector, a market we had cornered, were contemplating cutting their fees. In San Francisco, anticipating fallout from enterprise software start-ups, my partner Dee Anna McPherson suggested we change our start-up-focused strategy and instead go after bigger, more established tech companies. It was a very smart idea, but how would we go about winning *that* business? Would we even have time to implement this plan and be successful? Was it too late? I had to find answers fast and move quickly.

With so much change on the horizon, I knew that I needed to tighten things up and lower expenses, but I really wanted to avoid cutting staff. It all came down to cash. I needed enough to make it through a recession with no known end date. At a minimum, I knew my executive team and I would have to take salary cuts and forgo a year-end bonus so the staff could, just maybe, get a little something. The rest of the employees would take a smaller pay cut so that we could preserve everyone's job for a while. What's more, our line of credit at First Republic Bank just happened to be up for renewal—along with a balloon payment. I needed to renew that credit line and have it available as a safety net.

As all of this was happening, I also was in the process of hiring a new chief financial officer and was interviewing candidates. Unfortunately, none of them felt like a great match. I badly needed someone to help me navigate our financial situation. For the first time in seventeen years as CEO, I was feeling shaky—worried that we would run out of cash, afraid that it was all a house of cards. As they say, timing is everything, and I was running out of time.

Of course, no one could know that.

In the middle of these huge issues, there was day-to-day business. Client launches, staffing issues, employee reviews, and marketing all needed attention. Morale was low. The staff felt impending doom, and tensions on my leadership team were running high.

On Friday, I was supposed to go out on a date, but this was not the night for it, nor would it be for some time. My nanny, who made the world rotate for me while I worked and traveled for business, announced that it was time for her to move on to something new.

Walking to the Wall Street subway, I felt like I was wearing shoes encased in cement. I had just spent two hours writing everything down, compartmentalizing the chaos, and putting a straw man plan together. I would run it by my executive team the next day—get their input, guidance, and help. I silently prayed that no more shit would fall from the sky, went home, and made dinner for the kids.

Wonderful as they were, my ten- and seven-year-old daughters could not possibly understand the gravity of what I was dealing with at work, and my already worried employees didn't need to know that I couldn't work without someone to take care of my kids. I was unable to sleep and started taking Advil PM to get the rest I needed, a habit I sustained for ten years. I developed eczema and restless leg syndrome and drank way more pinot grigio than I probably needed to. To this day, I still sometimes wake up with my fists clenched, in fight-or-flight mode, ready for action.

I was basically in crisis mode for more than two years. I didn't recognize it because I didn't have time to think about myself, but, yes, that was a pretty damn lonely period, and it wore me down. I started to fake it, feigning interest in our prospects' businesses and my employees' career development. I was solely focused on getting the revenue. It wasn't fun anymore.

I was overwhelmed by relentless pivots and exhausted by a seemingly endless sense of urgency. My passion for my company turned into a grind, an exercise in just making it through one day after another. I didn't realize it, but others had picked up on it. At our annual executive planning meeting, my creative director, Mike Mancuso, said to me, "Sab, you need to get your swagger back."

He was right.

One day, and for no apparent reason, while crossing Second at Howard Street in San Francisco on my way to the office, I suddenly started to cry. That was my sign. Something was wrong.

CULTIVATE CONNECTION

Anxiety, isolation, depression, and loneliness are the occupational hazards of the CEO. Fortunately, there are things you can do to help yourself.

As a leader, you must make sure you have a range of go-to groups and people with whom you can talk and connect. This is crucial, but choose those people—and how you interact with them—carefully.

Leadership Team

Your leadership team may be the first leg in building a bridge over troubled water. Yes, your best ideas will always be better with their input, and yes, you want them to present diverse points of view and solutions. But above all, these must be people you can trust and with whom you can feel safely vulnerable.

Your leadership team is your inner circle, but you don't want it to become a bubble. The difference between a circle and a bubble is that a circle extends your effectiveness as a leader, leveraging your leadership connectivity, whereas a bubble insulates you and your team from the rest of the company and from reality itself. In a bubble, you start breathing each other's exhaust, and when this happens, you and your team will experience loneliness together, on a whole new, catastrophic level. Connectedness at all leadership levels is important.

Advisory Boards and Peer Groups

Company advisory boards, outside of your board of directors, meet monthly or quarterly with you and/or your leadership team and can help you with important business matters. They are composed of accomplished people who represent your company's circles of influence but without legal or fiduciary responsibility. They are consultants, former customers or competitors, suppliers, or partners. The thing is, if these people are worthy of being on your advisory board (and on your website), they will help to shape public perception of your leadership and your business. Like everything else about your business, these boards and groups communicate, and you need to be continually mindful of what they say in public.

I was at first hesitant when someone proposed that I join a CEO peer group such as the Founder Institute, Vistage, or YPO (the Young Presidents' Organization). Some peer groups may comprise members in your specific profession or industry; others are more diverse. Overcoming my doubts, I chose the latter. The truth is, I got the best advice and the most comfort out of those meetings. I made friends with CEOs from furniture, oil, and toy companies. It doesn't matter what industry you're in, or how big or small your company is; as a CEO, you face many of the same challenges. We validated one another's problems and gave one another solutions.

Coaches, Mentors, and "Silent" Personal Advisory Groups

Leadership coaches focus on the CEO mindset. With a professionally trained eye, they can be effective at creating unity within your team, channeling emotions, and focusing your thoughts. They have the benefit of knowing multiple leadership styles and organizational cultures and how they work together or don't. This is a paid relationship with an unbiased neutral third party, built for you and around you. It may be just what you need.

True mentors are people whom you've probably known for a while and with whom you have a strong personal history, such as a former boss or a retired executive. They have a vested interest in you because they've been in your shoes, have watched your professional ascent, and care about your success. They know your Achilles' heel and your various blind spots, and you can trust them implicitly.

The best coaches and mentors enable you to ask the dumbest questions or to spill your guts without regret or embarrassment. A ten-minute call with one of them is food for the soul. They will tell you what you need to hear, not what you want to hear. They will keep you from faking it. Consider forming your own informal personal advisory group with a combination of these people, outside of your company's other existing boards. You can count them on one hand. They will be the best support system you've ever had. I really can't stress it enough.

Your Physical Presence

Simply walking the halls can be an act of immediate connection. If there is a company function or office party, go to it. There's nothing more isolating than sitting alone in your office, hearing the laughter and music down the hall. But when you do go, don't unload on your employees or have one too many. Employees want a CEO who is open and approachable, yes, but mostly they want a leader who has their act together, whom they perceive as strong, and on whom they can count.

TEMPUS FUGIT

When you lose money, you can usually make it back. When you lose time, it's gone. *Tempus fugit.* Time flies. Irretrievably. Losing time squeezes you out of opportunities both professionally and personally, creates pressure, and generates more anxiety. CEOs are constantly competing against time in the search for windows of opportunity. You often feel that you are either cheating your business by spending too much time with your family or cheating your family by spending too much time with your business.

Balancing Work and Home

A lot has been written on the topic of achieving work–life balance, mostly targeting working mothers. Frankly, I gave up on it. I've come to believe that balance, as a state of being, is unachievable, because everything in work and life is dynamic, always in flux.

But I do believe in achieving moments of balance throughout the day by managing and rearranging priorities. Sometimes that moment of balance was a tiny escape: washing my hands with warm water and soap, centering myself as the warm water ran over my wrists, cleansing, calming, and soothing. I swear, it helped me reset and get ready for whatever was next in my day. It was my "Sabrina moment."

Life is not a balance sheet, and your employees, customers, and family are not line items. Your company deserves 100% of you, and so does your family. You created both of them. But the reality is that not everything and everyone can be equally important *all* the time.

Here's my take on it: everyone gets 100% of me—at the right time. At 1:00 p.m., my client is important. At 2:00, my employee is important. At 4:00, it's reading an important contract. At 6:00, it's catching up with my kids and making dinner, going to a parent–teacher conference, or helping with homework. When I make time to be with someone, I do my best to give them 100% of my undivided attention. That means keeping distractions at bay and trying not to read emails or text messages when I'm with someone. You will not achieve perfection at giving everyone your undivided attention. I surely never did. But, with practice, you can learn how to not cheat anyone out of their time with you. That, in turn, can at least make you feel somewhat balanced.

Of course, there are those times when you have to throw everything out the window because there's a crisis at work or someone in your family is sick. When you go to take care of the situation, just make sure you are *there*. One hundred percent. I thought nothing of making a one-day round trip from New York to San Francisco and back so that I could make it to Grace's annual mother–daughter soccer game or to Christina's school performance the next day. You do what you have to do, and you never think twice about it.

Meaningful Time

It is a good idea to divide your time even more finely. When someone talks about the importance of "me time," I think of this as cultivating outside interests—avocations, charitable work, study, a sport or other physical activity. If you have a passion to pursue, great. If not, consider rethinking "me time" as "meaningful time." Find an outside interest that genuinely absorbs and rewards you, perhaps work that builds on values relevant to both your business and your family. Speaking for myself, I find *meaning* more rewarding and rejuvenating than *me*.

OTHER WAYS TO FIGHT ISOLATION

Gratitude

Fostering a values-based work culture makes it easier to connect with the people in it. Celebrate your employees' successes and milestones. The mere expression of gratitude for their contributions is a powerful way to cultivate connection and reduce executive isolation. Every month, I handwrote cards to employees on their birthday or work anniversary. I started a mentor program to spend one-on-one time with aspiring employees. It was gratifying to hear about what they wanted to do with their careers, and it inspired me to help and support them.

Movement

When you're wearing those cement shoes, you feel stuck, overwhelmed by the enormity of the tasks at hand. Your tendency is to stay focused on what's familiar and remain caught up in the minutiae when what you really need is to see the big picture and get moving. Inertia is the CEO's enemy. If you get up inside your head too much and overthink things, you create anxiety. Over time, anxiety can turn into depression. And depression can be paralyzing.

Therefore, acquire a bias for action. Getting data to help you start to chip away at your problem is critical. Look to your advisors and mentors for help, and make an interim plan, even if you know it is not your best or final plan. A good plan implemented quickly is always better than the best plan implemented too late or not at all.

Pragmatic Optimism

A bias for action requires a bias for optimism. This is not to be confused with false hope or a denial of reality. When grounded in reality, optimism is a powerful leadership asset. Optimism is a belief in the feasibility of creating a future state that is better than the present state. In other words, optimism is forward looking, future oriented, and inherently strategic. In contrast, pessimism may feel realistic, but it makes you think about what you *can't* do rather than about what is possible. It is a mindset that resists change, promotes inflexibility, and diminishes resilience.

EMBRACE THE SILENCE

Up to this point, we have treated loneliness as an enemy. If loneliness is a kind of silence, understand that silence can foster insight and provide clarity. Embrace the silence; don't turn away from it. Distinguish between loneliness and solitude. As the existential philosopher and theologian Paul Tillich so instructively put it, "Loneliness expresses the pain of being alone [whereas] solitude expresses the glory of being alone." You may discover that solitude produces the most clarifying, purifying time you have. It is a precious gift, and one that CEOs rarely receive. Quiet time is thinking time.

Make it a priority to carve out time for silence—while commuting, walking the dog, exercising, being in nature, or after putting the kids to bed and before going to sleep yourself. Every week, I purposefully scheduled a thinking meeting with myself and put it on my calendar. Once in a while, I would leave the office early to think. Those cross-country flights were great thinking time, too. Something about being at thirty-five thousand feet opens the mind and gets the juices flowing.

As a CEO grows in both experience and in the role, he or she learns to use the isolation of leadership to free up and expand decision-making. It no longer hobbles your ability to make decisions and to act on them. Instead, you recognize the feelings of anxiety and make the mental switch. You learn how to push the little green man aside, replacing him with input from confidantes, new ideas, and small steps forward. You feel like maybe, just maybe, you've got this. With that feeling comes a quiet calm. It is the confidence that comes with seasoning in the CEO role, and it's a great place to reach. You're definitely not faking it, and you realize there's absolutely no need to.

THE PARADOX OF AUTHENTIC LEADERSHIP

It is true that close to half of a company's brand identity emanates straight from the CEO. Whenever you talk or read about a company, the CEO's name is usually in the first or second sentence. But here is the paradox: leadership, in practice, is always about everyone else.

If CEO is the loneliest job in the company, it is also the most selfless job in the company. As you grow in both leadership and experience, you will understand that the best leadership is not about you. The decisions you make, which are yours alone to make, are made for everyone around you. Even though you are thoroughly absorbed in these decisions, they are about doing what is best for the many and not the one.

To the extent that a CEO makes it all about himself, he is a fake, not a leader. After all, "Fake it till you make it" is about the person pretending to be someone he is not, while using others for personal gain.

Making it as a leader is about doing what is best for the company.

One year, when money was really tight and there was no financial rationale for distributing year-end bonuses, my leadership team and I gave our own bonuses to the employees. We took nothing for ourselves. This was a necessary decision for the company and therefore necessary for us all.

Making this decision was all about having faith in the future. All we needed to do was to think about the decision in a larger context and we concluded that passing up an immediate personal reward in exchange for the future of the company was the right thing to do. My employees gained from it, but so did we. And making that decision with my team during that holiday season was the least lonely thing I have ever done as a CEO.

CHAPTER SIX

AIRTIGHT

Let me share with you some of the most effective practices, tools, and strategies that I developed as a strategic advisor to our clients and as the leader of my company. My dual role meant that the problems I had to solve often overlapped, in both their nature and their timing, competing for my bandwidth. I realized I needed different approaches to either compartmentalize or integrate what lay in front of me. Moreover, I needed these methods to be simple so that I could quickly develop multiple strategies and play them out simultaneously, often with a lot of variables and detail.

The techniques I present here kept me focused in the midst of a sea of potential opportunities, obstacles, and hazards. Using them, I was able to produce options and make decisions I could implement with confidence when time was of the essence. I believe they can help you navigate multiple problems in parallel, deal with reality under pressure, and find your way even when your best-laid plans go awry. As a package, these techniques are management tools to help you run an operation that is airtight: efficient, strong, and resilient.

AIRTIGHT MANAGEMENT

As a marketing services firm, most of our work involved consulting with our clients through critical growth periods and around specific business events. There were countless strategy sessions, positioning workshops, company and product introductions, thought leadership campaigns, funding-round and leadership announcements, partnership deals and customer wins, acquisitions, mergers, and some very high-profile initial public offerings. We put their names up in lights, helped build their brands, created new industry categories, and lots more in between. In the end, success was a function of what our clients gave us to work with, brought to life by our creativity, insights, process, and relationships. As a service business, we achieved this in the context of three immutable vectors: people, money, and time.

As CEO, I was naturally focused on leading and managing my own firm. With my leadership team, I navigated the friction of business expansion and contraction within different groups and across locations. We also innovated our services—for example, we were one of the very first agencies our size to offer corporate social media strategy—and positioned our firm as an industry leader. We had to evolve our own brand to stay fresh and in front of the competition. Success was a blender of anticipating shifts, identifying obstacles, and making the right decisions based on our core values, against those same three vectors: people, money, and time.

In business, as in life, it can be easy to overcomplicate things. The shortest distance between two points is a straight line, and I tried to find that straight line. The key was to achieve simplicity that was compatible with the complexity of the issues at hand. To do so, we built plans—strategies with tactics, each in anticipation of the next strategy or tactical move. And because business is always in flux, we constantly adjusted those plans, gravitating toward the path of least resistance.

This was particularly important during tough stretches as a wartime CEO. Knowing there would be obstacles, we hunted for them and got them out of the way early. If solving one problem would create three new ones, I had to solve that problem differently. The bottom line was that, with fewer twists and turns, we could be more efficient and nimble, spending more time winning business and pleasing our clients. This, to me, felt like a smooth operation, a tight ship. It's what I call airtight management.

When your operation is airtight, you're quite literally squeezing the daylights out of the places where your values and vision come into contact with strategy, and where your strategies end and tactical execution begins. These gaps can be very hard to find and squeeze out. Done right and relentlessly, airtight management eliminates the cracks through which careless mistakes, hidden agendas, and other vulnerabilities can creep. It encompasses critical management functions, from planning, problem-solving, strategizing, and decision-making to how you communicate and work with your leadership team.

MY FATHER SAID IT BEST

There are a lot of great quotes about the value of planning. "If you don't have a plan, you don't know where you're going," my father used to say. "What is more," he would add, "you probably don't know where you are, either." When you are running a million miles an hour leading your organization, it can take a very deliberate act of self-control to pause and put a plan together. Your impulse is to move and get things done. But a good plan, even a straw man of a plan, is the basis for everything you do, a menu of strategies and tactics stapled to a road map. A lot of thinking should go into putting that plan together, and volumes have been written about how to do it.

Often forgotten in all that thinking, though, is the reason for the planning in the first place.

I can't tell you how many times a tech executive has said to me, "Sabrina, we want some PR for our company" or "We want to be the leaders in artificial intelligence–based data recovery software platforms for Fortune 500 financial services companies." Or when an employee would say something like "We should go after the biotech market" or "Let's redesign the break room with couches so we can take naps!" Modulating my excitement for their enthusiasm, my response was just two words: "Great! Why?"

WHY ARE WE DOING THIS?

Getting the answers to *Why are we doing this?* is a key first step in realistic planning. Planning involves asking *what* and asking *why*, but, to borrow the title of leadership guru Simon Sinek's 2009 bestseller, *Start with Why*.

The beauty of starting with why is that it opens the door to a host of other essential questions, such as *Is this a must-do or a nice-to-have? Does this support and enhance our brand promise? Is this the right market for us to tackle?* and *Do we have the resources to pull this off?* Going through the *Why?* exercise is critical to making the right commitments, identifying need, uncovering pitfalls, and shaping and executing a strategy that will benefit your company while still being in alignment with its brand. Sometimes it's enough to make it clear you're not going to proceed at all. Or you might give it a quick test, or table it until certain conditions exist.

Asking why helps you find the cracks in your initial thinking, and sealing those is a critical first step in airtight management.

WHAT DOES SUCCESS LOOK LIKE?

What does success look like? is the second most critical planning question. By answering it, you identify key goals and objectives. As the iconic minimalist architect Ludwig Mies van der Rohe put it, less is more. One of the biggest mistakes young companies make is to spread themselves too thin with too many initiatives, causing them to lose sight of their core. Instead, focus on three or four primary objectives within any fiscal year.

Ask yourself, *One year from today, what will we have accomplished?* In the process, consider outputs versus outcomes. Sales leads are very different from actual sales. Actual sales are very different from a customer realizing their return on investment. Describing what success looks like, and being able to measure it, are vital to keeping you on track.

Between *Why are we doing this?* and *What does success look like?* you should see some interesting alignment. With these ends of the spectrum in place, it's easier to begin to fill in the middle.

STRATEGY + TACTICS = EXECUTION

Coming up with an idea is easy. You can have a stroke of genius in an hour, a minute, even less. Making it come to life—that can take months or years, and sometimes it never happens. Many companies fail because of poor execution. Often, they pick the wrong approach, or they run out of money, having spent it on tactics, with not much to show for it. Great execution is a function of having a plan with the right strategies and tactics supported by the right resources.

Strategy flows from values, vision, and mission—your brand. It is your blueprint, approach, and plumb line through space and time. Tactics are the tools of the moment, the touch points that flow from strategy, connecting it to reality. The magic of a great plan is how strategies and tactics match each other, meshing like the gears of a fine watch. Tactics must align with strategy for an idea to be realized in the real world. It should be a one-to-one, tongue-in-groove, hand-in-glove kind of relationship. Finding that alignment and keeping it airtight is how an authentic CEO runs an efficient operation and a successful business.

During the 2008–2009 recession, we had three strategies. I kept them simple so everyone could remember them:

1. Sell like hell. (Win business.)

2. Keep what we've got. (Retain clients.)

3. Protect the core. (Preserve culture while managing expenses.)

The tactics for each of these strategies revolved around business development, client service, and our culture and finances. What did success look like? Coming in with flat growth at the end of the year, with a (very) small profit, and with our core clients and employees intact seemed like appropriate goals. The reason why was obvious: so we could live to fight another year and ultimately thrive, not just survive.

The complete ecosystem in which authentic leadership takes shape encompasses brand, strategy, and tactics. No CEO can successfully fake their way through this ecosystem and expect to build and support an enduring enterprise. It is impossible to successfully implement a reality-based strategy with faulty tactics, just as it is impossible to be successful with the wrong strategy supported by the right tactics. The tactics themselves are as authentic as the strategy they serve, and that strategy is as authentic as the values, vision, and mission that stand behind the brand. This is one powerful trifecta.

At the same time, we know that business is fluid. Markets evolve, and new competitors move in. A great plan is not a "set it and forget it" kind of exercise. Strategy and tactics must be resilient through inevitable change, yet flexible enough to adapt to the reality of change. If, along the way, you're doing something that's not helping you achieve your goals, you shouldn't be doing it.

THE HOCUS-POCUS OF FOCUS

If you are a CEO running a young company, you have to stay focused on your bread and butter, your core business, which is, after all, what got you started and what's keeping the lights on. Such focus is key to the solid execution of a business plan and should mirror the objectives you've set forth in your plan. But as a business matures, you discover that macro and micro forces are constantly at play, swirling around you. They distract your focus, presenting opportunities and challenges even as they more urgently prompt you to protect the core. I call this the hocus-pocus of focus (figure 4).

To be competitive, you can't just look down the hood. You have to look down the road, and across both sides of the street. Maintaining a laser focus fixes your concentration but can blind you to hazards looming ahead, as well as to the most promising opportunities, which often take shape on the periphery. Yet you cannot allow yourself to be overwhelmed by undefined "opportunity," the next new thing, beyond which there is inevitably yet another new thing. The risk is taking your eye off the ball, diluting or damaging your core business.

I struggled with this over the years, and it often was costly. There were several tech bubbles (other than the first Internet boom) when we took on a few too many new clients and couldn't staff up fast enough to support them. This compromised service to existing clients. Employees quit because they were stretched thin with too much work. Then we lost a few of those existing clients too because, well, there were even fewer people to work on their accounts. Ultimately, it was like running in place, but with some dents in our reputation. We lost our focus on preserving a great work environment and a culture focused on doing great work.

Then, as the markets started to shift, I ignored the signs and, with the best of intentions, opened a satellite office or made a really expensive strategic hire or invested in market-specific research tools that we wouldn't need in the long run anyway. Inefficient and sloppy, it was anything but airtight.

I had to save my company (and myself!) from these agonizing situations. I had to be able to avoid becoming unduly distracted while *also* being open to new opportunities or hazards.

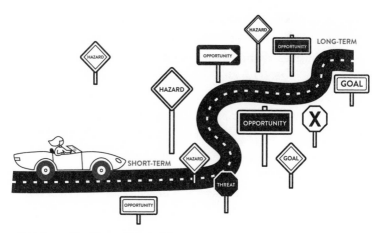

FIGURE 4   The Hocus-Pocus of Focus

Before you start driving toward your objectives, consider creating a near-term outlook, which guides what you do every week and month, as well as a longer-term outlook, which never loses sight of ultimate goals. Together, these combined outlooks force you to pay attention to every milestone along the way, so that each move you make is in anticipation of the next.

Beyond this dual depth of field, you need both narrow-angle and wide-angle vision. The narrow angle zooms in on your target, and the wide angle takes in the periphery. Being this vigilant requires the discipline to keep your head down and your eye on what's in front of you even as you continually develop awareness of what is on the horizon. A self-prescribed safety net of sorts, this can help you detect elusive opportunities and threats and fill those cracks before they appear in your foundation.

The examples of my own company's expansions and contractions represent some of the scenarios that CEOs of emerging growth companies classically face. The right strategy in all of these situations is to recognize and comprehend the trends proactively—that is, in time to either capitalize on them or avoid them. This is key to running a successful business. Get out in front of potential growth opportunities that can advance your company, but sidestep the pitfalls that may put you in a compromising situation, hurt you, or even kill you. Focus is magic when you are vigilant and resilient, because it enables you to look both straight ahead and around the corner.

WHAT'S MISSING FROM THIS PICTURE?

In our practice, we constantly interacted with business reporters and research analysts, some of whom were the toughest pros in the industry. They were successful because they asked the hard questions in search of the truth. The best ones were able to uncover fakery in product viability, company strategy, and financial statements. How? They were naturally curious. But they also looked for what was missing. They didn't take much at face value, poking holes in what they saw, digging further.

An important part of planning and decision-making in leadership is to look beyond basic explanations and to instead find what is *not* there. Identifying what's missing is more valuable than what you can see right in front of you, especially when it comes to making really big decisions. It's that little nugget, that little extra 5%, that distinguishes what may be great from what is merely good, or the long-term triumph from the short-term flash in the pan. Things that are missing can be hidden under many layers, or are complicated, or rarely occur. Other times, an important fact may be intentionally buried, shoved under the rug. Those are the facts you *really* need to find.

Great CEOs and leadership teams play devil's advocate with their own plans and decisions. I was fortunate to have people like that on my team. We poked holes in one another's ideas, not to deflate them for our own satisfaction but to be sure they truly made sense and were in the best interest of the company. In essence, we made sure they were airtight. Looking for cracks and faulty seams in a plan is also like playing detective. You ask the same question five different ways to see if the fifth answer is different from the first four. Furthermore, something as simple as asking open-ended questions, as opposed to yes-or-no types of questions, can be helpful. For example, asking "When does this product not work well?" might give you more insight than asking "Does this product work in all these applications?" Or, "This strategy sounds great, but what could go wrong, and what if X or Y or Z happens?" will give you more meaningful input than "Do you like this plan?" To get unbiased input, effective leaders run their plans by people who aren't involved in company planning or strategy at all. They consult with their employees and personal advisors. And they study the research their people find for them.

All business plans and strategies are imperfect. Your job as a leader is to make them less imperfect by looking for the disconnects and gaps. Poke your plan full of holes, and then plug them back up until every exception has been dealt with.

SPINNING PLATES AND PLANS

Plans are essential, but almost all of them suffer from a bias toward linear thinking. Plans are intended to bring order to chaotic thought. The trouble is, we tend to equate order with a linear progression and chronology—a beginning, middle, and end. Plans are flat. But a flat plan will only guide a CEO so far.

Reality exists in three-dimensional space plus the fourth dimension, time. Everything is always in flux. Being a CEO requires you to establish yourself in time and space, which means handling multiple problems and opportunities, at their various stages, with their own moving parts and details, all at the same time.

Remember the plate spinner who appeared on old TV variety shows? His entire act was to keep an impossible number of plates of different sizes and weights spinning on sticks to the music of Khachaturian's "Sabre Dance." Clearly, that plate spinner wasn't operating from a flat plan. He couldn't impose a rigid sequence on the plates he kept spinning. By watching multiple plates at the same time, he had a fair chance of keeping most of them spinning.

As a CEO, a leader of a group or division, or a leader of anything, really, *you* are a plate spinner. It's damn hard to manage the plethora of initiatives, issues, problems, and aspects of business simultaneously. So how do you keep all of your plates spinning?

THE "MAKE IT HAPPEN" BOX

The Make It Happen box is a three-dimensional box or cube, a mental map I developed to help me multitask like a boss. It is a way of visualizing three essential functions—compartmentalizing, sequencing, and parallel processing—to organize chaos, prioritize, solve problems, develop strategies, and activate all three functions simultaneously. The Make It Happen box evolved symbolically out of years and years of being challenged by countless clients ("Can you guys just make this happen?") and by our own audacious goals ("We need to make it happen!"). To make *it* happen, I needed a way to quickly map out *how* we were going to achieve the goal we had signed up for.

Using the Make It Happen box, I can manage the issues on my own agenda while accommodating a daily influx of new ones. It keeps me from feeling overwhelmed and preserves my clarity of thought. Moreover, it helps me identify potential options to navigate a situation or make a decision. It helps me capture all the relevant aspects and details of a scenario so I won't be surprised later by something I missed.

Mental mapping works well in the big picture because it lets you run several often conflicting business issues or strategies side by side. For example, in PR and other service businesses, resource allocation—matching people to work—is always a problem. The issue is that you can't hire a whole bunch of people in anticipation of business you might not win, but you do need the people to win the business—and you'll need them instantly, once you've won it. You must recruit constantly, looking for good people at different levels in parallel with winning business, so that, somehow, you'll have the right people with the right expertise and skill sets at the right time.

That's a lot of different plates to spin: existing staff; a variable workforce; ongoing recruiting; different levels of skill sets, expertise, and seniority; fluctuating periods of activity; the sales pipeline; new business; and existing business opportunities. Of course, you're also spinning plates on other critical initiatives, such as your geographic expansion strategy and your vision for where your company is headed, or a partnership deal you're working on and product line extensions. Each of these has its own issues, variables, timetable, obstacles, and requirements.

To break it down, here's how the Make It Happen box works.

Compartmentalize

Take a piece of paper (in a pinch, a cocktail napkin will do) and draw a three-dimensional box or cube. Inside it, write down the name of one of your initiatives or an issue you need to solve. Next, on each side of the cube, assign relevant labels, variables, people, contingencies, and even emotions (figure 5).

For example, when I had to get my arms around whether to close our Boston office, I drew a cube and wrote "Boston" inside. (Putting it inside somehow made the issue feel more contained and manageable.) On the left side of the box, I detailed out staff and employee factors I had to consider. On the right side, I outlined our current client and business development situation. On the front, I jotted down leadership issues. On the back, I put reputational issues. On the bottom—because the bottom line is always on the bottom—I listed the financial issues I had to consider. On the top, I wrote down how I felt about the whole Boston situation (sad, emotional), together with how others might react (angry, disappointed). Finally, extending out from the box, I wrote down external

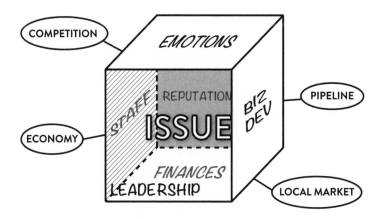

FIGURE 5   "Make It Happen" Box Example

factors impacting the business, including the state of the economy, the local Boston market, and competitive factors.

Everything about that scenario, all the primary issues associated with it, were on that box. It felt good to see it and to have it all in one place.

Sequence

From here, I created two new boxes. One was called Stay; the other, Go. I started to break down and play out each scenario in greater detail. If A and B occurred, then C and D would need to happen. I filled in each side with the requirements, steps, and risks inherent in the situation.

To elaborate a bit, the left side of the Stay box included finding new office space, signing a new lease, and other considerations involved with moving. The right side included rebuilding a client base, potentially in other tech sectors, and researching those markets. The front detailed our professional, operational, and leadership requirements, and the bottom, the financial costs and risks—especially in light of an impending recession.

The Go box was easier to fill out and took less time. It basically meant leaving our space, supporting Boston's client business out of New York, giving the remaining staff the option to relocate or work from home, developing a practical and empathetic communication plan to inform everyone, and using the remaining funds in the budget as a cushion should the economy go to hell in a handbasket.

There was of course much more detail than this, but you get the idea. In going through this exercise, sequences started to emerge. The actual order of events and the requirements to make each of them occur became clear. I then circled those sequences and numbered them. I wrote how I felt about them and how others might feel.

To be sure, this is not a very scientific cost-benefit analysis in risk management, but I was under some serious time pressure, with other urgent issues to attend to. Going through this exercise was all that I needed. With it, I had netted out all the major issues, found a couple of viable options forward, and identified the upside and downside of each. I then took my recommendations to my executive team for further input and discussion.

What clearly emerged was that effecting a smooth, graceful transition out of Boston and folding that office into our New York operation outweighed taking on the obstacles and risks involved in trying to achieve continued success there, especially in light of the economy. It also helped me to deal with the emotional factors that were impacting my ability to make a decision.

Sequencing everything gave me my rationale and strategy. Next, I needed an action plan to carry it out. I needed a process.

Process

The process piece is all about tactical execution: who is going to do what, when, how, and to what end. Here, you take your cube and just extend out each side with those variables, identifying dates; key people and teams that can help; documents that had to be written; key messages, notifications, and assignments. As events unfold and new information emerges, the path may bend, changing the order of the process. That is fine. The main thing is that you *have* a process—a strategy you have already thought through and can run with—all on one piece of paper. One of the worst feelings in the world is being confronted with a decision for which you are simply unprepared. You don't have anything up your sleeve. You feel anxious. You can't move. You can't execute. The spinning plates are starting to wobble and fall.

You can use the compartmentalize–sequence–process approach to deal with multiple big issues happening all at once, as I had to do when closing an office while ramping up revenue in another, and renewing our line of credit while finding a CFO and hiring a new nanny. But this process also comes in handy on a micro level, as a mental map, just to get through a busy day, especially when personal and professional lives collide, which they have a habit of doing.

MULTI-MICRO PROCESSING

All on one day, my incredible partner of seventeen years, Shannon Latta, told me she needed to move to France for family reasons, my daughter Christina broke her elbow in gym, we were pitching a huge account that I needed to be in, a client was going public on NASDAQ, I had a big planning meeting to decide on our future information technology infrastructure, and my father was put in hospice care. None of this appeared to be sequential. Everything appeared equally urgent. But if everything is urgent, nothing is urgent. There is no valid excuse to avoid prioritizing.

I mentally organized the day by putting it into an imaginary cube, with each event taking a side. Isolating the events but keeping them together in the box made them manageable in my head. Each event had a different level of emotion, importance, and time horizon associated with it. An order of priority began to emerge. Labeling how I felt helped me contain and control my emotions so I could think clearly.

Attached to each side of the box were the two or three things I absolutely needed to accomplish *that day* to move those events forward in the right way. I had to make *them* happen. I processed the events and tasks through my mind to their ultimate outcome. I could give 100% of my attention to each critical situation, toggling back and forth between them to nudge each along. Anything else—hundreds of emails, the "Hey, Sab, do you have five minutes to talk?" chats, conversations, decisions—could wait until the evening or the next day. This enabled me to plot out each move in anticipation of the next. Sequences and pathways emerged.

Deploying several sequences in parallel is most emphatically *not* trying to think and do everything at once. Instead, it is about creating parallel tracks and keeping multiple large projects, initiatives, and goals moving forward simultaneously, but always on their own track and without conflicting. Here's how that day, in particular, played out.

My client rang the bell in the NASDAQ studio at 9:30 a.m., and I could easily handle a few of the CEO's press meetings until 11:30. In the taxi en route to the sales pitch at noon, I called my mother to console her and spoke to the hospice facility to discuss my father's care. I made a note to check in again at night.

During a bathroom break in the middle of the pitch, I emailed Shannon to ask if she thought running specific aspects of the firm from abroad was feasible and if she could put together an outline of a plan *that* day. By 2:00 p.m., I learned about my daughter's injury. I excused myself from the meeting, which, thankfully, was finishing up anyway, and took a taxi home (the local train would have taken too long). In the car, I researched orthopedists, made the emergency appointment, and called our nanny to tell her to meet me at the hospital.

With that in place, I called my IT guy, explained my predic-ament, asked him to send me his presentation to review that night, and rescheduled our discussion for the next day. A delay of one day would not impair our IT implementation plan.

By five o'clock, I was in the emergency room getting Christina's arm in a sling and scheduling her surgery, and then I took a glance at Shannon's draft plan in the waiting room. Utterly relieved that it looked like something that could work, I called my client to congratulate him on a successful IPO (initial public offering). The stock opened higher than expected, went up to $28 a share, and held. The press coverage was good.

I emailed my prospect to thank him for the opportunity to pitch their business, asked for feedback, and followed up with my team. After dinner, I was able to say a few words to my father, who appeared to be okay, checked in with my mother once again, read more documents, and caught up on email.

About half of my days as CEO were like that, some with larger or smaller crises or events. There were Speed Racer trips to the airport, many highly stressful moments, and, at the end, exhaustion. Sometimes I had so much going on that I had to re-compartmentalize and re-sequence multiple times a day to see things through. The key was being able to roll with it, spinning those plates in real time, taking great care to break as few as possible. As long as I could compartmentalize, sequence, and process, however imperfectly, I felt empowered to handle whatever was in front of me. I didn't stick my head in the sand, delay, pretend, minimize, or otherwise feel the need to fake it. True, I could not always control everything perfectly, and there were definitely times when it got (really) messy, but I was able to stay grounded in reality and ultimately became more resilient. Bottom line: I was able to *make it happen.*

DEALING WITH CRACKS IN THE ARMOR

Aiming for a business that's airtight means maintaining dynamism within discipline. Your leadership team, who they are and how you work with them, is central to your mission and the success of your business. As we grew, I had different leadership teams, each with world-class people in the industry. If you're fortunate, *your* team consists of people you trust to explore and evaluate whatever you cannot. They amplify your vision by letting you look through their eyes. Sharing authority with them multiplies your power. But when the final decision for action is made, the discussion and debate must stop and all divides must be bridged. Everyone must align on the chosen plan of action and get behind it. Standoffs are not an option. You need unity within your team, and unified support, to proceed.

Unfortunately, leadership team alignment may not always be possible. In these cases, it is vital to agree to disagree, and as the top dog you have to ask for commitment before moving forward. In such situations, you must truly take your colleague's concerns under advisement. Agree to pause often at designated checkpoints to evaluate whether the plan is working or going sideways, discuss it together, and make changes if needed. Listening to concerns, reflecting upon what team members tell you, and being grateful for well-meaning warnings are central to maintaining team cohesion, and *that* is key to running any successful enterprise.

There are fewer things more poisonous than unresolved issues, resentment, and distrust within a leadership team. Left to fester, these create a culture of politics and divisiveness that ultimately destroys company values and impairs brand integrity. It is critical to take the time and effort to get to the bottom of conflict and resolve it, or failing that, to part ways justly but quickly.

Whatever you do—the tactics you devise, the action you choose in the moment—must flow from your enduring values, vision, and mission. You, your company, your brand, are not what you say they are. They are what you do. That is worth remembering.

CHAPTER SEVEN

LEADER AND *LOSER* BOTH BEGIN WITH THE LETTER *L*

Any book on leadership should consist, at minimum, of two parts: one on winning and the other on losing. The great majority of these books don't venture past part one. They focus mostly on winning, with some advice on how to avoid making mistakes.

The reality, however, is that you will make mistakes, and plenty of them, no matter how many books you read. To be a leader is to lose—more often than you would like.

That feeling you get when you know you negotiated a bad deal, missed the quarter, let the troops down, and generally failed, is like no other, especially when everyone is counting on you to lead them to victory. Bottom line? It is really hard to act like a leader when you feel like a loser.

Let's explore how to recover from failure, how to organize your thoughts, communicate effectively, and begin to put things back on track. How you come back from being a loser says everything about you as a leader. With time and practice, you will become more resilient. It might even keep you from making those mistakes again.

NO CEO IS BULLETPROOF

No matter how airtight your organization is, or how experienced you and your leadership team are, you will make some mistakes. You will make bad decisions. You will also make perfectly good decisions that produce bad results or worse. Sometimes people who work for you will make mistakes. Those mistakes may not be your fault, but they are your problem, because they happened on your watch and you need to help fix them. Other times, unfortunate things will just happen that are out of your control. Whatever the scenario, you can always count on the timing to be bad.

No book or consultant or management guru can make you bulletproof. No leader is perfect, and even the best CEOs can't dodge every bullet. But they can develop the skills to quickly regroup, restrategize, and live to fight another day. Effective leaders are resilient. They can stand in the middle of any disaster, find the least disastrous path through it, and come out on the other side, ready to bounce back.

Resilience pays dividends in endurance and confidence. It also throws in a bonus: Being resilient keeps you from faking it. It's like a shield. In your resilience, you realize you have no need to fake it. You've got this. There *is* a solution, and you *will* find it. Being resilient helps you make it.

How do you develop resilience? Going through the wringer enough times does give you a thicker skin. You've been to that rodeo before and you know how it's going to play out. As Gina Pacheco, our receptionist in San Francisco for many years, used to say, "Got the T-shirt, got the hat, got the key chain."

Experience teaches you that failures are *temporary setbacks* from which you can recover quickly. That's what makes you resilient. You bounce back. You take responsibility, analyze what happened, ask the right questions, learn, provide a path forward, communicate effectively, and set expectations. But most of all, you know—because experience has taught you—exactly when to move on. Those who are resilient have a bias for action. They don't wallow. They learn and then move on, beyond failure. They put it in the rearview mirror, where it belongs.[1]

OLYMPIC TEARS

The scene is IBM's corporate office in Armonk, New York, at 1:00 p.m. on a clear Friday in April. We are pitching IBM for the 1996 Olympics information systems account, a prestigious piece of business. Winning it would put my five-year-old firm in a different league. We would be playing with the big boys, and if we did a good job, could win other big, brand-name tech clients.

I had flown in from San Francisco on a red-eye, just turning around from an intense four-day press tour for another client. In those days, press tours were like IPO road shows: a dozen in-person meetings per day with top analysts and reporters to introduce a new company and its products. Running on adrenaline and two hours' sleep, I went to a Kinko's in Queens, New York, to make copies of my overhead slides. We had gone all-out on those overheads, printing in color for the very first time (a big deal in the mid-1990s). The Olympic torch was a vibrant orange, and the Olympic rings appeared in their appropriate Olympic colors.

I was so proud of those overheads as I carried them into what must have been the shabbiest room at IBM headquarters. There was an overhead projector but no screen. We had to project our beautiful images onto a corner wall, which contorted the words, making them awkward and hard to read. At the appointed time, we were asked to begin, even though the key decision maker had not yet arrived. When the big guy finally walked in, halfway through our presentation, he scowled at the odd presentation setup (as if it were our doing!) and flipped impatiently through a printout of the deck I had given him.

"Where are your *big* ideas?" he asked, interrupting me. "Just tell me your big ideas. What is your strategy? Where's the budget? I don't see the budget!"

In rapid fire, he asked one question after another, giving me no chance to answer any of them.

I could have stood up to Mister IBM, could have told him he missed *our* big ideas because *he* was late. Or I could have pointed out that the shithole of a room *his* people had put us in wasn't big enough for our big ideas.

But I had lost control of the meeting. I had lost control of myself. I was suddenly so profoundly exhausted and rattled, I could not move. Standing there, looking down at my beautiful slides on the overhead projector, I started to cry. My tears dissolved the vibrant orange ink of the Olympic torch, bleeding into the black typed words to form a trail of ugly brownish liquid. It was all so grotesquely visible, projected, onto that corner of that miserable room.

The IBMers started glancing up at the ceiling, looking for leaks, as my teardrops continued to fall onto the bed of the slide projector. My colleague Elizabeth Orgel stood up, came over to me, and said gently, "Sab, I think it's time to go."

She led me to the bathroom, where I sobbed into the very hard paper towels I pulled, one after the other, from the wall dispenser. The only salvageable part of the day was drinking a good deal of chardonnay on the flight back to San Francisco. But then Elizabeth got the stomach flu and was incredibly sick for most of the six-hour flight.

For me, this experience remains a vivid memory of defeat. I had humiliated my firm and myself. But the fact is that it really happened, and you can't fake yourself out of feeling like a total loser. You can't fake yourself out of crying on your slides—or, for that matter, of throwing up on a plane.

NO EXCUSES

This story has no surprise twist. We did not get the account. It was failure, flat out. But that did not mean it was valueless. If you face failure, you have to own up to it and analyze it. You might find it is rich with useful lessons.

I had failed *so badly*, I decided to do a formal postmortem, an investigation into what had happened and why. Like the National Transportation Safety Board sifting through the wreckage of a 747, I was hoping to find things that would prevent an Olympic-size disaster from ever happening again. Don't wallow. Learn.

I recommend doing a postmortem every time you make a big mistake or experience a big failure. Always include everyone who was involved in that failure, so that they can contribute and learn from it, too.

- What happened?
- Where and when did it go off the rails?
- What should we have done about it in the moment?
- What could we have done differently/better before?
- What have we learned?
- How should we proceed now?

The value of this exercise is that it makes you face reality and keeps you from laying the blame elsewhere. When you lose a big sale to your competitor, it's easy to say, "They won because their account manager is dating the prospect" or "They got the deal because they brought out their big guns from New York and put on a whole show for them." The truth is, while relationships and stunts do matter, intelligence, insights, creativity, passion, and sheer effort can matter more. You lost, not because of what *they* did but because of what you *didn't* do.

This is the level of exploration and development that real leaders encourage, ask of themselves, and ask of their people. (By the way, I also recommend doing an after-action report following a big win, to understand and potentially repeat what went well, what you did differently, and the circumstances under which you were able to succeed.)

In our case, I learned to never again let desperation replace strategy. Yes, the guy from IBM was a jerk. Yes, they gave us a terrible room to present in. Perhaps we were doomed from the start. But I also could have exerted more control of the situation from the start.

I *should have* insisted that IBM respect us, provide a proper conference room, and have everyone show up on time, or reschedule the meeting. I should have simply stopped, gotten hold of myself, and put the toe tag on the meeting.

"It doesn't seem like this is a good time for you to be hearing our presentation, so perhaps we should reschedule for another day. We can come back and present the ideas you have asked us to share."

That's what I should have said, and then politely excused myself and my team. On a personal note, I also should have managed my calendar better and not pushed myself to the point of exhaustion before such a critical meeting.

Would they have invited us back? Hell, no. But we would have stood up for our brand. We would have demonstrated how highly we valued ourselves and our services. We would have extracted from the experience at least a fragment of a moral victory. And I would have personally upheld my own integrity. After all, it is integrity, accountability, and emotional stamina that make a CEO durable. Had I done this, I might not have ended up in tears, though I suspect that Elizabeth still would have gotten sick on the flight home.

TAKE RESPONSIBILITY
AND PROVIDE A PATH

You might think that, as an executive, admitting mistakes shows weakness, but handled in the right way, it actually shows strength—strength in your integrity and accountability. It makes you more human and builds trust through transparency and the vulnerability of admission. It therefore helps you to build a culture of shared ownership that is nearly immune to politics, resists passing the buck, and frowns on fakery.

As a leader, the buck stops with you. Your company's, division's, or group's mistakes and failures are yours. Own them. The people around you—your shareholders, employees and teammates, customers, whoever is being affected by the blunder—need you to do this, and they respect it. But just being transparent about a mistake is never enough. People want a lot more. They want a solution, a fix, an improvement. A mistake should trigger a solution, a road to something better. Set a plan for improvement, turning adversity into advancement.

You certainly can start with "I'm sorry," but you can't ever leave it there. Claim ownership of the problem, apologize, and with your very next breath reveal the path forward. Find a way to make it better than before. Go back to the postmortem you conducted. This is how you preserve and defend your authenticity, your brand, your reputation, your everything. Here are a couple of examples.

Scenario A

WHAT HAPPENED? The marketing campaign plan we implemented did not produce anywhere close to the sales leads we had promised. We missed the goal by x%.

WHY DID IT HAPPEN? First, we had a slow start and did not achieve momentum soon enough. Second, we did not produce enough of the right kind of content with the frequency that the campaign needed to be successful.

WHAT'S NEXT? We have identified a new resource with some fresh ideas inside the company and will give the campaign another try for two months. Based on results at that point, we should fish or cut bait. Here is the new road map . . .

Scenario B

WHAT HAPPENED? I have some difficult news. I'm sorry to say that we lost the Big Kahuna deal to Competitor X.

WHY DID IT HAPPEN? Upon review, we did not do enough research into Big Kahuna's future expansion plans, our pricing was off, and we did not address a crucial element of their request for proposal. I take responsibility for this because I now see that our company needs to devote more resources to large, complex RFPs.

WHAT'S NEXT? Effective immediately, we are forming the Big Kahuna RFP SWAT team, consisting of Joe and Tania from the product development group, to help us improve our win rate with these larger opportunities. Here is what the go-forward plan looks like . . .

WHEN THEY'RE JUST NOT THAT INTO YOU

Life isn't fair sometimes. There will be those days when you brought your A game and your A team, where the terms of the deal were perfect, there was great chemistry, you crossed your *t*'s and dotted your *i*'s, and you *still* lost.

Maybe your prospect was told by his boss to just go with the bigger, more established vendor, the "safe buy." Or perhaps they loved your extended product offering but, in the end, your presentation helped them see that, actually, they just need a smaller solution. And then, my personal favorite: the prospect's CEO wanted to work with the firm she worked with before.

There are situations where there's just no winning. You can't fake your age or your size or manufacture relationships you don't have. Stay grounded, align around your core values and mission, and remind your team what you stand for. There is a reason why you and your people work at your company, and why other people don't. Losing in these situations can be a blessing in disguise. The wrong partnership could have crushed your company, the deal might have been excruciatingly difficult to customize, or the hire might have been a terrible cultural fit.

Again, you don't want to make excuses for what you didn't do, but you can call a spade a spade, learn from the experience, share that information, and then—quickly—move on to the next opportunity better suited for you.

SETTING EXPECTATIONS

Entering any new market, going after bigger fish or lots of smaller fry, means you will face new competition and different customer requirements. It is a conscious decision for which you have, it is hoped, done enough research to get you adequately prepared. But the reality is that you may lose more deals than you are used to losing, especially in the beginning. The sales cycle could be longer or harder, unexpectedly impacting your overall quarterly revenue. The key is to make allowances for the unknown and then to set and communicate realistic expectations accordingly.

Setting expectations early to avoid disappointment later is an important exercise, but also a delicate one. You want your people to feel confident going in, and you want to carefully choose who on your team is best suited to drive the effort with you. Yet you can also set the stage *anticipating* that the initial phase will come with some surprises. What you learn from the initial phase can be used to sharpen your approach and to win more over time. You also can set more reasonable, frankly conservative targets than you otherwise might. This isn't planning for loss or faking it by minimizing expectations to make outcomes look better. It's being realistic about a new situation.

The point in all this planning is that less than optimal outcomes do not necessarily mean that you or your people have to *feel* like losers or that you are less than optimal. Prepare for whatever results may come by communicating the proper perspective. Losing can ultimately be part of winning.

ASK, AND YOU SHALL RECEIVE

When problems come to you in search of a solution, the common expectation is that you, as the leader, will have all the answers. We have talked about how even the best CEOs don't always have the right answers, but they do have the right questions. "Knowledge" consists of knowing what you know and what you don't know. This is the inflection point at which the curve either bends toward fakery or finds another direction. Instead of trying to fake it till you make it, realize that *nobody* ever has all the answers and that you alone can't fix everything.

Good salespeople make the case for their merchandise by explaining benefits, features, and price. That's a push, and it can provoke a sale. But *great* salespeople get their prospects to talk about what *they* want and need. Great salespeople push with the right questions, and that can pull from the prospect the knowledge needed to close the sale. The best sales pitch is neither an explanation nor a declaration. It is a question. Sometimes lots of questions. It becomes a conversation and a relationship. Its objective is to hear the voice of the prospect, the customer—the voice of the *other person.*

Every successful communication converts *your* push into the *other's* pull. This communication tactic is a catalyst that activates any sound strategy. In my career as a CEO, I used it often, and it got me out of the loser corner many times. It is based, more or less, on three little words: "Tell me more."

ME: *(after an extensive presentation of ideas)* What do you think of our proposal?

JILL THE CLIENT: I hate it. This is just not what I was
    looking for.

ME: (*avoiding the temptation to appear defensive or
    offended*) Oh? Tell *us* more, Jill. What exactly is
    turning you off?

ME: (*after listening to and discussing Jill's issues*) Thank
    you for explaining all of this to us. It's really useful.
    I have to ask, if there's still an opportunity for us to
    come back to you with a different proposal, would
    you be willing to entertain that?

Here's another example:

JIM THE GROUP DIRECTOR: Sab, I just can't get behind
    this bonus plan. No one in my group likes it. So I'm
    just letting you know that we are going to go with a
    different bonus plan.

ME: (*hiding my irritation at Jim's total disregard for our
    compensation program*) I'm sorry to hear that. Tell
    me more.

JIM: It's an old-fashioned plan. It's not very incentivizing
    and not inclusive.

ME: (*wondering if it's just Jim who doesn't like the plan
    or if it's really his group*): Okay, can you elaborate?
    I'd like to get the CFO involved, so we can agree on
    something that works for everyone and our budget.

COMPLAINTS ARE GIFTS

Objections, negative responses, complaints—all of these are
gifts. They need to be unwrapped. Responding defensively only
sacrifices the knowledge the person confronting you is trying to
give. Instead, listen. Maybe you will find out how to do better.

Push with the right questions and you will pull that knowledge out of them.

In the examples above, and in most human interactions, people ultimately just want to be heard and understood, even though they may not go about it in the best way. As a leader, you must separate yourself from the emotions coming at you and focus instead on your goal. In the end, you may not be able to do better, and you may not be able to convert the loss into a win. But what you *will* have accomplished is far more important. You took the time to preserve, protect, and maybe improve a business relationship precisely when it was critically stressed and potentially ready to head further south. Inviting or continuing a discussion shows that the relationship has not yet broken.

At the very least, you have protected your brand. Customers talk to other customers and employees talk to other employees. Word gets out. If you fail to hear their voices, you can be sure that word of your failure will spread to others. "I hate it," "This sucks," and "We don't like this plan" are opportunities to prove that yours is the brand that listens, hears, learns, and always strives to be better. That alone will carry you further than any one deal you may have lost. That is endurance and resilience. And that is business success.

WHAT GOES UP DOES, FOR A FACT, COME DOWN

There was a period in our New York office when we won a new account every week. It was incredible. We became the go-to agency for any viable company in the very hot advertising technology sector. In San Francisco and in Boston, there were also years when literally 100% of our business came to us through our network, all referrals from VCs, board members, CEOs, and marketing executives. As a firm, we were in the very fortunate position of being able to choose which companies we wanted to pitch. It was hard work, long hours, and it paid off. Across the board, we won far more often than we lost. It was great!

Until it wasn't.

Markets go through cycles. They consolidate, morph into new markets, or make a comeback later. The economy, of course, also has its cycles. During such cycles, fewer leads are coming in, the competition is tougher, and it can be harder to win. Markets notwithstanding, there are times when your sales presentations might just not be as fresh or as impactful as they need to be or you didn't come across as hungry enough for the business. It was raining, your lead person called in sick, and you just weren't feeling it. Whatever the reason, the losses become more frequent.

Along your journey as an executive, you may find yourself on a losing streak. When losing a deal that was yours to win falls hot on the heels of two or three other losses, you start to wonder if you've lost your mojo. Your people might start to feel like they are working for a loser company. Morale erodes, and the same old pep talk sounds like a broken record.

"We've hit a losing streak," I would say. "Every company goes through one."

I had to pop the loser bubble and redirect the energy to something new.

"I know you want to feel like you are part of a winning organization. No one wants that more than I do. Winning is up to everyone. Let's figure out how to get things back on track."

In our leadership team meetings, we problem-solved. We widened the circle of involvement beyond ourselves and our most senior teams to the rest of the staff, broadening our knowledge base. Everyone was asked for their top three business development ideas, and groups were formed in each office to lead the charge—in the right direction. We hired outside consultants. We also drew up a client survey. I spoke to clients directly and asked them, "What can we do better?"

Among a few other things, I learned that we needed to sharpen our social media expertise. We were an early leader in social media strategy, but our offering had become a little outdated. We also needed to get out there in a more modern way. We put together a sizzle reel of our recent work. We synthesized our skills and expertise into three markets where we had connections, and our teams in San Francisco, Boston, and New York went after them.

While we were always able to turn the corner, we sometimes found ourselves repeating history. What I realized was that those losing streaks were, in part, a function of getting a little too comfortable while we were enjoying our winning streak. It's what generals call victory fever. I wasn't looking down the road or across the street. All along, we should have been deploying some of the strategies I mentioned above, or at least applying them more frequently and proactively, rather than waiting to drag them out in response to a problem already well under way. The moment I focused on feeling like a winner, I put my blinders on to losing, and thereby let it creep in.

This was a hugely valuable lesson. When things are going well, almost too well, that's exactly the time you need to start planning for what's next. Losing can clobber you when you are already losing, but it can really sneak up on you when you are in the lead. This is another reason why achieving and maintaining a market leadership position for your company is so hard. There is no place to go once you get there, except down. Part of being a great leader is never losing sight of the possibility of losing. Such is the very thin line between loser and leader. After all, they both begin with the letter *l*.

CHAPTER EIGHT

WAY OFF THE MENU

As a communications agency, we were frequently called in to help our clients manage their crises. Data leaks, product defects and delays, missed quarterly earnings, executive shenanigans, canceled mergers and partnerships . . . you name it, we handled it. When the wheels were coming off the client's bus, we stepped in, helped them get to the bottom of what actually happened, formulated a communications plan, and found a path forward.

As an executive of an organization, whether large or small, it is not a question of *if* but a matter of *when*. You *will* face several crises of varying severity, consequence, and pain during your career. Even though every crisis is different, there is a basic framework to manage them, which I'll share here. Suffice it to say, the best damage control starts with planning, long before any crisis ever occurs, so you are better prepared to act when it actually hits.

Different types of crisis plans—contingency (preparation for business disruptions), disaster recovery (restoration of vital support systems), and business continuity (survival after a crisis)—are industry specific. Many crisis plans include contingency, recovery, and continuity all in one, and a lot of larger corporations are required to submit them to their boards and governance committees. Regardless, a top executive at *any* company should be well aware of what plans are already in place and, if they are not on the shelf, should make a concerted and urgent effort to create them. This said, it is alarming how many start-ups and emerging growth companies don't have any crisis plans.

As CEO of a communications firm, I had the unique experience of having managed crises for my own company as well as for our clients. Somehow it was always easier to help someone else with their problems than to deal with our own. While I had "seen it all" for my clients and had a few what-if scenarios of my own to draw upon, nothing could have prepared me for what I learned one windy day in November 2012.

Picture it. I was in a New York taxi en route to see Mike Perlis, CEO of Forbes Media. Our firm was handling the communication strategy around their digital publishing brand transformation and I was meeting Mike for coffee to discuss it. I was coming off a brutal couple of weeks, dealing with the impact of Hurricane Sandy—a crisis unto itself—on both our New York–based business and my own family. Expecting a decline in fee income, I had already lowered our forecast for 2013. This exposed our expenses—which, as I reviewed them, seemed oddly high to me. I decided to investigate.

Somewhere close to Fifth Avenue and Fourteenth Street, the financial statements I requested a few days earlier landed in my email. It was all there, on my tiny smartphone screen. The gist of it was that a trusted employee and longtime friend—a person who had been a guest in my home—had embezzled up to half a million dollars over a period of several years.

A concoction of emotions—shock, anger, betrayal, shame, panic, relief, fear, failure, loneliness, and embarrassment—hit me like a tsunami.

This is really happening, right now, I thought. *This is not a bad dream, and there is no faking any of this.*

In fact, it was number two of a one-two punch, extremely hard to absorb on the heels of the financial hit we were just beginning to take from Hurricane Sandy. What's more, we had only recently recovered from the 2008–2009 recession. I mean, it was not as if we wouldn't need the half million. The investment of time and pain involved in the untangling of this mess loomed like a tumor, massive and shapeless. This definitely had the power to kill my company, our culture, and our reputation. How I managed this would be of the gravest, utmost importance.

In the actual three minutes remaining of that cab ride, I had to internalize what I had just discovered, process my emotions, and then somehow magically pull myself together for my meeting with Mike. I stuffed it all into a brand new Make It Happen box and shut the lid. I paid the cab fare, put on a smile, and walked into the coffee shop. It was that simple and that hard.

WHAT DOESN'T KILL YOU . . .

In my experience, crises fall into three main categories (figure 6). They all have the power to ultimately severely damage, even kill, your company, depending on how you handle them.

Category A and category B are similar in that they are events you think will never occur because they are *unthinkable.* Hardly standard fare, these are way off the menu. They don't happen often, but when they do they usually feature the element of surprise and move quickly, with sweeping and potentially devastating impact. Category A crises are external events that happen *to* your organization, such as acts of God, terrorism, serious economic recession, or, more recently, a global pandemic. They have nothing to do with you but have the power to wipe out

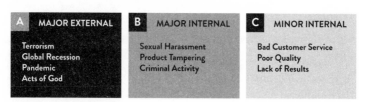

FIGURE 6   Crisis Categories

your business, your industry, or human life. Category B crises are internal to your organization, were born there and festered on your watch. These include things like criminal activity, sexual harassment, product tampering, and so on. They can be just as destructive to your company's long-term survival as the crises of category A.

Not to be underestimated in their destructive potential are category C crises—call them mini crises. These are more frequent, run-of-the-mill business problems that, left unattended, can become bigger crises and pack serious long-term consequences for business health. On the typical menu of business fails are systemically bad customer service, poor product quality, and an overall lack of results, among other items.

In all crises, it may be tempting to fake it. You may not fully acknowledge the crisis, may decide to minimize it, or may fabricate some or all of the explanation about how or why it happened. Yet, at the same time, nothing shatters the fake it ethos more completely than staring a crisis in the face. Successfully engaging with a crisis, no matter what kind, is partly a function of how prepared you are to handle it. For category A and B situations, this is crucial, because so much can be at stake. For category C situations, other safety nets and frameworks can be put in place.

Unfortunately, I was not as prepared as I should have been to deal with Hurricane Sandy (category A) or employee fraud (category B) because, of course, I never thought they would occur. I should have been taking more of my own medicine.

PEA SOUP

When Hurricane Sandy hit New York on October 29, 2012, our offices at 55 Broad Street, down the block from the New York Stock Exchange, were massively flooded. All of Lower Manhattan had been hit really hard. We occupied the twentieth floor, but the elevator shafts were submerged in seawater, which corroded their wiring, worsening the damage by the hour. There was no way to pump the shafts out into the already flooded lobby and streets.

Working from home almost anywhere in the tri-state area was virtually impossible for several weeks because of extensive cell tower damage and sporadic electrical outages. The homes of a couple of our employees were flooded and uninhabitable. Every client had marketing plans and important corporate announcements hanging in the balance, delayed, or canceled. The phone, had it been working, would have been ringing nonstop. It was a mess, and there was a lot of confusion. I was working with Ben Billingsley, my partner in New York, and our priority was to somehow get the majority of our employees safely back to work so that they would be able to help our clients.

On November 4, a Sunday night, I was able to contact a few friends, including Dave Moore, CEO of 24/7 Real Media; Jeanne Sullivan, partner at StarVest Partners; and Wilma Jordan, CEO of investment bank JEGI. I asked if some of my employees could work out of their less hard-hit midtown Manhattan offices for a few days until our Internet and Wi-Fi came back online.

They proved to be friends, indeed. I dispatched my employees to their temporary venues, and they went about supporting their clients through their own respective crises. We put our two displaced employees into hotels until they could get back into their homes or find other places to live.

Every day, Ben and I iterated our plan in progress and provided staff and clients with regular updates on the situation. The team exchanged information about their personal situations and comforted one another. Overcommunicating was essential. We built trust with that plan, and folks came to rely on our updates even when the status remained the same.

By Wednesday, November 7, some of us were finally able to get back up to the twentieth floor and into the office. The Internet was still down, but the cell towers were humming, so we all sat in our biggest conference room, made use of our personal hotspots, and did email and client work.

On Monday, I went back to my "wartime" CEO, laser-focused plan from the 2008 recession. For a second time, it came down to this: sell like hell, keep what you've got, protect your core. Our sales pipeline would undoubtedly be affected, and there was a good chance that contract renewals for 2013 would be delayed. We would need to get aggressive and creative. I sat down to lower my fourth-quarter forecast and adjust the 2013 budget. That's when my antennas went up. Why was our travel and entertainment budget so high? What were all these additional expenses?

With that awful feeling that something was very, very, wrong, I worked with our finance team and contacted my advisor Darryl Salerno to do the forensics. The fraud had essentially occurred through fake expense reports that had been doctored to pass through years of credit card charges. My fears were confirmed during that taxi ride to see Mike Perlis. It was pretty simple, really, and frighteningly easy to pull off. Every night after dinner, my daughters helped me match the fake charges on the fake expense reports with the real charges on the credit card statements.

At that point, I dropped everything and focused 100% on the situation, moving and pushing the process along as rapidly as I could, with a lot of help. One week later, the week of Thanksgiving, I had a detective from the fraud unit at the local precinct assigned to the case, confronted and fired my former friend and employee, received a written admission of guilt, and processed legal documents for financial remuneration. Make no mistake, there was a ton of work involved, including the review of thousands of accounting records, conversations with an assortment of lawyers, and the preparation and review of many documents. It was intense, and there was no time to reflect upon how I personally felt about it. Finally, there was figuring out what to say, if anything, and to whom.

Being a privately held company, I was not required by law to disclose the fraud. So I had a decision to make. Would it be in the best interest of our employees and our clients if they knew what had occurred? Would they somehow benefit from having this information? Had the fraud materially affected them, or would it in any way impact them personally or financially going forward? I had no legal obligation, but did I have a moral one? Was *I* faking it if I didn't disclose this terrible event?

While I believe being forthcoming and truthful is vitally important, I am also pragmatic. I was running a business. Had the crime affected my employees or clients, I would have been morally compelled to disclose what happened, with or without any legal requirement to do so. Since this was not the case, the benefits of providing the news on a need-to-know basis far outweighed the downside of sharing this information broadly.

With the support of our attorney, I chose to handle the matter quietly, communicating the news and recovery plan only to those whom I was indeed obligated to inform: my partners and extended leadership team, advisors, and board. I knew there would be internal chatter, but I much preferred to take a possible hit for lack of transparency than to risk damage to our culture, clients' potential loss of confidence in our firm, or a leak to the industry through the press. That kind of scope creep would have created a much, much greater problem for my company—including my employees and my clients—and would have meant a much longer and more difficult recovery. This time, though, I *did* create a contingency plan, together with prepared statements, in the event that an extended crisis were to be the unfortunate case.

The cleanup and general aftermath of this crisis were huge distractions. It was a cloud hanging over me and the others involved in the process. We ultimately recovered financially and put new protective checks and balances in place. I also learned that my company was hardly unique in suffering this crime, that employee fraud occurs rather frequently and to varying degrees, often without ever being detected. Not that this knowledge made me feel any better. The entire episode took its toll. It attacked my confidence and it made me doubt myself.

Had *I* been faking it? After all, I had somehow allowed this to happen, in my own company. Here I was, taking so much pride in running a tight ship, when all along there had been holes in my hull. Were there more? What else did I not know about? Was I an incompetent CEO for failing to see the warning signs sooner? Was I a terrible person for failing to anticipate my employee's criminal act? Could I ever trust any of my employees again? Clearly, I would never be "friends" with them, not ever again. I had been taken for a ride.

PLAN AHEAD

I speak from experience. The worst time to develop a crisis plan is during a crisis. Your hands are more than full. Stuff is flying at you every second. You are too busy responding—implementing, acting—to draw up a careful plan. Having preemptive crisis plans tailored to the possibility of a global pandemic, cyberattack, war, lawsuit, catastrophic earthquake, or internal fraud is not an unreasonable precaution in the world in which we live today.

As a CEO, working through multiple scenarios like this will make you think differently about your company, how you run it, and what you choose to invest in. It might even help you to avert a crisis altogether. At a minimum, it will help you navigate the chaos more effectively, if and when it happens.

A Framework

Crisis planning should go hand in hand with business planning. What you need is a set of straw man plans, templates, hypotheticals, checklists—whatever you want to call them—and you need them at the ready. The best plans outline the protocol, communication responses, mitigation processes, and recovery procedures for any given crisis. They won't seamlessly match any actual crisis, of course, but they are blueprints and foundations from which to operate. They will keep you from feeling—and reacting—like the proverbial deer in the headlights. Here is an example.

- **Scenario.** Explain the potential crisis. Clearly state what has happened and what is happening now. Break down the scenario if there are multiple components.

- **Vulnerability assessment.** Outline the risks and impact of the scenario on every aspect of your business and on every affected stakeholder. Consider the ripple effect and the chain reaction of damage.

- **Communication protocol and spokespeople.** Identify the core team of three to four people that will manage the crisis. Designate who will be the *lead and only* person to speak about the crisis. Source any third parties you might need for further support and data. Be sure you have the emergency contact information for everyone involved.

- **Plans of action.** Outline potential steps and actions you could take to disintermediate the crisis.

  - What is the recovery plan to resolve the crisis? You should have two plans: one that is short term, an urgently efficient procedure to put out the fire, and one that is longer term, to rebuild things to be more fire resistant, if not fireproof. All aspects of your business must be considered here.

- Though the situation may be disastrous, what are reasonable outcomes? What could success look like? How will your company move forward?

- **Questions and answers.** Put together a list of potential tough questions you might get asked about the crisis scenario. These would be questions from employees, investors, customers, and the press. Prepare concise answers in response to them. This may bring up points you want to factor into your overall plan. Make sure your legal counsel is involved in the review process, and arm your leadership team and spokesperson with that document.

Acting It Out

It is important to set aside time with your leadership team and board of directors to review and update this crisis plan. Depending on your business and the volatility of your industry, this might happen every six months. Talk through each crisis as if it were a live event. In playing the scenario out, get used to stating the facts in the way you've seen law enforcement officials do on the evening news. Ask people how they feel about the situation. Talk about those feelings and acknowledge them now so that they may be less likely to cause panic later.

Important as it is to lay out the problem, it is equally important, maybe even more, to switch quickly to finding and implementing a solution. Lay out the steps to move forward—to contain the crisis, to resolve the crisis, and importantly, to move beyond the crisis. The future is always where it's at.

Of course, when a crisis is actually unfolding, your plan will be subject to rolling revision in real time. Successfully engaging with a crisis calls for compartmentalization to keep things running (there are those spinning plates again) while you also formulate and deploy—simultaneously—multiple strategic responses. And you do all this against a backdrop of swirling debris.

You can't anticipate every way a crisis could go, but if you think through a worst-case scenario ahead of time and have a set of procedures for dealing with it, there is reasonable hope that you and your company will come out the other side. And you won't be faking it. Being realistically optimistic, if you are prepared, you can face a crisis with the confidence of knowing you can resolve it.

POSTMORTEM

At this point, you may wonder whether I would have handled things differently had I prepared in advance a template plan for each of my two crises? The answer is yes, and in hindsight the steps seem mostly obvious.

In the case of Hurricane Sandy, I would have made sure to keep an updated contact list of my employees and clients at home (this was made available, but I did not have it on hand). I would have made those phone calls for a little help from my friends— whom I would have already identified and listed—more quickly. I would have purchased backup emergency technology solutions in advance and perhaps would have been able to get my employees back to work sooner. I also could have saved time in financial scenario planning by having a plan B budget on the shelf and ready to go, and by identifying in advance other potential business strategies, or by activating certain sources of revenue.

In the instance of the employee fraud, I could have instituted checks and balances as part of the contingency planning process, which actually might have prevented the entire event from ever occurring, or at least limited the damage. For instance, I could have had our books audited by an outside firm, something which, as a private, closely held business, I was not required to do and which I chose to avoid as an unnecessary expense. I will never know this for certain, but I do know that having a plan in place would definitely have given me more confidence. It would have forced me to address my feelings about it, which could have helped me manage my emotions more effectively and kept me from feeling quite so rudderless. Mostly, it would have saved precious time in thinking things through, in figuring out whom to ask for help and how to reach them, and importantly, how to secure faster financial restitution.

The irony of these two completely unrelated crises is that the first, Sandy, brought the second, the embezzlement, to light. It took the loss of business from the storm and the floods to prompt the kind of financial review that exposed my employee's fraud. That, in turn, made me stop and resolve it. Without the catastrophe of the hurricane, who knows how much longer the fraud would have continued or how much worse it would have been? I suppose I could consider this fragment of serendipity the silver lining in two catastrophic events from *way* off the menu.

RULES OF THUMB

In the *middle* of an actual crisis, I have found that certain rules of thumb generally apply. The most important is that *you don't have to have all the answers, but you must always have a next step.* Forward motion is key. Succinctly formulated, the rules look like this:

1. Never say anything you do not absolutely, positively know to be true. Honesty is the best policy, and it is the only policy available to you. Bad information, like squeezed toothpaste, is impossible to put back into the tube. Truth may evolve as a crisis develops, so add new information as you get it—but only as you get it. Don't make predictions, and never give false hope.

2. If the situation is due to something you did (or failed to do), you must admit it, own it, and explain it. Then talk about next steps and how the situation will be corrected. You cannot change the reality of a current crisis, but sometimes you can assign that reality a new meaning, recasting it into a new and hopeful future.[1]

3. Get help from accredited outside experts if needed. Show that you are cooperating with them and are following instructions.

4. Set realistic expectations and try to exceed them. I'm not suggesting that you set the bar low, but it's always better to underpromise and overdeliver.

5. Promise timely updates and deliver on them. Keep people in the loop.

6. Appoint only one spokesperson. A bevy of "authorized" spokespeople saying even slightly different things creates confusion and distrust. You can, however, designate a third-party subject matter expert to address specific points, provided you are aligned.

7. Don't hesitate to be repetitive in giving instructions. People need to hear things more than once and through multiple channels, especially when they are being personally affected by a crisis.

8. Always keep your communication simple and direct, using pictures and visuals whenever possible.

9. Reassess the status of the crisis every day. Review any progress or new damage uncovered and revise go-forward plans as needed.

10. Rinse and repeat.

In my twenty-four years as a CEO, I experienced four macro-scale category A crises: the Internet bust of 2000 to 2001, the attacks on the World Trade Center in 2001, the recession of 2008 to 2009, and Hurricane Sandy in 2012. In terms of impact, the Internet bust and the recession were serious socioeconomic crises, while 9/11 and Hurricane Sandy were in a tragic class by themselves. All caused injury to my company.

The COVID-19 pandemic that began in 2020 struck after I sold my business and was no longer its CEO. But we need to mention it here because it brings the demands of crisis planning to a whole new level that is unprecedented in our lifetimes. We business leaders must understand that the effect of pandemic disease, climate change, and even levels of political instability most Americans never before contemplated are now part of our crisis portfolios. We must be prepared for the wildest scenarios and the most eccentric gyrations of business. With COVID, almost everyone had to shift, without any preparation, to conducting business and learning entirely online. We should also now imagine and prepare for a world in which all online communication and commerce might suffer devastating attack and generalized disruption, necessitating a fallback to "anti-quated" brick-and-mortar business practices. Hard to imagine, but indeed possible.

My category B employee fraud crisis of 2012, which obvi-ously was contained within and impacted *only* my company, was nonetheless equally capable of destroying it. These were each (I would hope) a once-in-a-lifetime, once-in-a-generation, or even once-in-five-hundred-years event. But I am hardly alone in experiencing five such crises in my career. Such events are, sadly, common, and part of our reality today.

IF IT'S NOT ONE THING, IT'S ANOTHER

While full-blown catastrophes are impossible to ignore, it's the everyday problems of business that are easy to let slide. Like a pimple on an elephant's butt, they are hard to notice in the big picture of things. They are the daily *drip-drip-drip* of cumula-tively corrosive problems: lapses in service, human mistakes, poor performance, and bad judgment. The damage they cause is often stealthy, gradually eroding your business. None of them cries out to be solved, but that is what makes them so dangerous. Meanwhile, since you have bigger fish to fry, you assume that other people will take care of these problems or that ignoring them will somehow give them space to just go away. Cumulatively, these micro fails can become injurious crises for your business. It can become death by a thousand cuts.

Here are three typical category C situations, with responses that might seem familiar.

- **Situation 1.** A big customer is unhappy. She is being nice about it, but she's mentioned it twice now and no one has gotten back to her. *Response:* Oh, it will be okay because she's always been easy to work with.

- **Situation 2.** Last week, a couple of employees were in the elevator talking about some insensitive language one of your managers used in an email. *Response:* Don't worry, they were laughing, so it probably wasn't a big deal.

- **Situation 3.** Your new product is off to a slow start because the marketing material kind of sucks, and your salespeople are using an old deck. *Response:* Meh, it's an easy sell, so they will be able to pull it off.

Left unchecked, here's how these scenarios might play out, six weeks later:

- **Situation 1.** Your customer has defected, leaving you for your competitor. She lost her patience and decided to post her feelings about it on social media, which is reaching other customers—and other prospects.

- **Situation 2.** Your human resources manager received a complaint demanding your manager's removal, and your approval rating on Glassdoor is now at one star, reflecting your company's tone-deaf culture.

- **Situation 3.** Halfway through the quarter, sales are 15% below where they should be.

Seemingly nonurgent, or even stealthy, as such issues are, they *must* be attended to. Remember: complaints are gifts, but doing nothing is a threat. The first order of business is to create the structure, an auditing system or feedback loop, whereby problems surfaced by stakeholders can be addressed in a timely fashion. With that in place, there is no excuse for you, or some designated member of your team, to fail to resolve these matters. Just remember: if it crosses *your* desk, *you* need to make sure it is dealt with.

THE TROUBLE BUBBLE

You may have your own method for dealing with these kinds of issues, but the point is to have something that works. The goal is to minimize the number of problems you have to solve so that you can focus instead on opportunity, growth, and business success.

Ben had a great process for dealing with category C matters, which he shared with me every week. It was a process he had institutionalized as a way to catch issues before they became problems, and problems before they turned into bona fide crises. He sorted each core aspect of his operation—clients, staff, revenues, ongoing initiatives, and so on—by its current status. Most were "good," but others were in what he called the "trouble bubble." The name is reminiscent of an old board game called Trouble, where you pressed the bubble in the middle of the game board to throw the die, which determined how far you could move your game piece (figure 7).

The trouble bubble metaphor was a way to isolate and focus on a problem. It was a way of compartmentalizing it—not for the purpose of keeping it at bay but to give it space in which it could be observed. This was where Ben and his team could do triage and apply remedies to the most urgent issues, solving them with immediate action. As for the more complicated problems, we would plot out a strategy and course of action.

Here, we would refer back to a simple but highly effective methodology that we had codified to make sense of complex

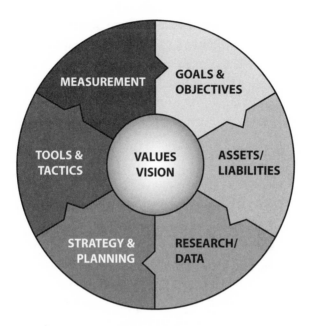

FIGURE 7   A Planning and Troubleshooting Methodology

problems and to create campaigns for clients. It helped us to get back to basics and identify the root cause of a problem. Sometimes the key was the revelation that the goal had changed, or that we—or our client—had lost sight of it. Other times, extenuating circumstances changed our original strategy and a new angle or more information was needed. The power of the method was its simplicity. It was based on some straightforward questions:

- What is the overarching objective and what does success look like? What are interim goals we can achieve?

- What do we have to work with that can help us? What are our assets? What is working against us? What are the liabilities? What could go wrong?

- What is missing and what research do we need to conduct?

- What are all the strategies at our disposal to solve this problem and achieve our goal? How do we put them together into a plan for maximum impact?

- What are all the tools and tactics we need to execute on those strategies?

- How do we measure and monitor progress? What levers do we look for to improve or pivot in a different direction?

THE TROUBLE WITH PEOPLE

Problems in the service industry are always people related. Problems in the product industry are product related, but all products, even those built by robots, are ultimately created and used by people. Everything begins and ends with people.

"If it weren't for the people, everything would be easy!" my fabulous partner in San Francisco, Debra Raine, would say.

The problem is that you cannot *control* people—cannot *fix* people—any more than you can control or fix the roll of a die. But you can usually exercise some influence over the outcomes of what people do. You can lead by example or manage performance. You can coach and guide. You can understand and empathize. You can just simply listen. And you can communicate.

DIFFICULT CONVERSATIONS

How you communicate with a person about an issue, problem, or crisis can be the difference between success and total failure that leads to an even bigger crisis. During my career, I've learned fifteen important tips that can help any leader in a tough situation:

1. Consider the right place to have the discussion. A neutral location is always best.

2. Leave your emotions and ego at the door. Nothing will kill your chances of a successful outcome more than even the hint of anger, fear, or excessive enthusiasm.

3. Communication is rooted in psychology. Take time to understand the background and modus operandi of the person with whom you are talking. Communication problems often are not the result of what you are saying but of how you are saying it.

4. Begin by expressing your desire to resolve the matter at hand. Always begin with a positive message.

5. Be honest and direct. Tell the truth, but take care to separate a problem from a person, and then address the problem rather than the person or (worse) the person's personality.

6. Be very clear with yourself about where you want to end up. In proposing solutions, make sure that you can live with whatever options you suggest.

7. In challenging situations, consider interim steps as short-term solutions and progress goals.

8. Again, those three magic words: "Tell me more." When you don't know how to respond or to answer a question, when you're being attacked, or when the other person is stalling, get them to talk more. The more they talk, the more information you have to make your next point.

9. Reflect upon how the person is feeling and coming across. Repeat what they have told you, if necessary. Validation is very powerful.

10. Watch your reaction to an obvious ploy. "I don't know how to interpret that" or "I don't understand what you mean" are viable responses to stonewalling and sarcasm.

11. Be comfortable with silence. It can help you connect better. Make sure the other person knows you are listening.

12. Welcome criticism and be grateful for it. It is useful data, even if it is untrue, because it's something you can use later to make an even stronger point.

13. Use the other person's name when making your points.

14. Consider your body language. Is your body turned toward them? Are your hands and arms unclasped? Gestures open? Posture tall (not slumped), yet comfortable?

15. If the discussion becomes hostile, calmly reiterate that you wish to resolve the matter at hand and then propose that you find another time to reconvene.

. . . AND DO IT WITH GRACE

As a CEO, you must always hold your whole business in your mind, on both a micro and a macro level. No matter how intense things get within your four walls, the bigger picture must always loom larger. This is a chief reason why being a leader is hard.

On the seesaw of business, you want to be somewhere in the middle—hypervigilant, straddling both the worst and the best, seeing what you want to accomplish and what lands in your lap, aware of both the problems and the solutions. This means being observant, paying attention to a wider circle of the world, checking your gut, and managing the day-to-day risks to protect yourself from danger. The fewer obstacles there are in your way, the more you can focus on the future. The more prepared you are to deal with these obstacles, the faster you can achieve your business goals.

In the great circle of business, one such goal (and it is the ultimate goal) is transacting your business—turning it over to others, selling or merging it, or perhaps taking it public. This is the subject of the final chapter.

CHAPTER NINE

THE FOUNDER'S CURSE

If you have founded a company, you have a singular relationship with it that is unlike any other, defined by the emotional tie, the commitment, and the passion you have for your creation. This is the same bond that develops between inventors and their inventions, authors and their books, carpenters and their woodwork. CEOs who take command of a company also forge a very intense bond, even if they are not the actual founder.

Still, in no person is this almost blood tie more powerful than that which binds a founder with her company. The devotion a founder feels for her business infuses everything, from its culture and processes to the snacks in the kitchen. It is the sheer will to succeed and to survive catastrophic crises that would bring others to their knees.

The emotions a founder feels are awesome, but there is also a downside. Such devotion can blind you to everything that's wrong with your company. It can impair your judgment and objectivity, preventing you from hearing what you need to know.

It can affect your ability to make the right business decisions in a timely manner. It's like faking it, but on a whole different level. This is the "founder's curse."

Anyone with an intellectual, emotional, or spiritual ownership stake in an enterprise can be touched by the founder's curse, but if you are the literal founder, your business may feel like your baby. Of course, it is not. Your children are your children; your business is just business. But the emotional attachments are surprisingly similar.

Your child is always yours, but you also understand and accept that you raise your child to someday lead an independent life. You may have trouble letting go, but you know that you must. Likewise, the business you created is always yours. You will always be its founder. Yet you must be able to let go and sell your business when the right circumstances present themselves. You also have to be able to step aside and let someone else take the reins when that is called for. For personal, leadership, and business reasons, these are very delicate and challenging matters.

University of Southern California professor Noam Wasserman, author of *The Founder's Dilemma*, warns of the tendency for company founders to outlive their usefulness. Many stay on long past their "sell by" dates, refusing to release the reins they have held from the birth of their company.[1] This can impair a company's ability to scale, limiting its growth to the founder's interests and skill set. In a worst-case scenario, the passionate entrepreneur works hard to achieve tremendous success, only to be removed by her investors and replaced by a new leader who goes on to manage what she has accomplished. The founder is damned if she is successful and damned if she isn't. Exiting your own company in this harsh manner can have terrible financial and emotional consequences.

Consider a company that grows from zero to $10 million. It needs a certain kind of leader who can get things off the ground, articulate a vision, create a culture, get initial funding, build and launch a product, and find a market for it. But when that same company grows from $10 million to $100 million and beyond, it needs an executive to grow a sales organization, manage multiple functions, deal with customers, develop strategic partnerships, navigate acquisitions or potentially take the company public, and handle the financial complexities of a more global entity. These are two very different skill sets, and while it is not impossible, it is unlikely that the same person will possess both.

SUCCESSION PLANNING

A founder's longevity is a more common issue than you might think, and a very hard truth to face. This is why executive succession planning, though so important, is frequently over-looked, especially in tightly controlled founder/CEO businesses and family-run businesses. It should, in fact, take place early in a company's life. Depending on the incorporation and ownership structure of your company, consider doing the following:

- Hire a personal attorney to draw up a founder's employment agreement, which might include an accelerated vesting and a severance package. Make sure you have a clear plan around your vesting schedule and agreements around a possible termination or company exit.

- In your business plan, identify a role within your company that you might assume at the right time in the future, such as moving from CEO to chief strategy officer, chief evangelist, or chief product officer. Your choice should play to your strengths, preserving values and vision while making room for new leaders.

- Investigate mechanisms to obtain some liquidity of your founder's equity in connection with a venture-financing round.

- Create strong stock option plans or other equity ownership/ phantom stock programs for key employees (executive and C-level or partner-level staff), which are transactable in a public offering or sale.

- Set aside two or three common seats on your board when incorporating the company, to provide breathing room and maintain some level of control. Carefully fill those empty seats only when necessary.

- Establish and remain on good terms with your investors and board members.

REMOVING THE CURSE

The best entrepreneurs and founder/CEOs don't try to fake it and can instead be honest with themselves about their skill sets and value. Introspection is vital to planning. Here are some questions to ask yourself when considering your ongoing role and thinking about the future:

- What does the future of my company need from its leadership?

- Am I still cut out for this job, and do the needs of the business match my skill set?

- Am I still having fun in my job? Do I still have the energy for it?

- Is what I'm doing providing value, and is that still an important function in the business?

- Can I help achieve my company's goals next year? In two years?

- Am I increasingly coming into conflict with what others are doing in my company or how others are changing my company? Why is this happening?

- Is it time to groom someone else to deal with the challenges that lie ahead?

- Is it time to reevaluate my own role?

- If I'm not doing this job anymore, what am I going to do? And how will I feel about that?

- What do I want out of my contributions here? Is it financial reward? Prestige?

Also important are checks and balances, such as performance reviews with 360-degree feedback from board and advisory members, leadership team members, and colleagues. I have always believed in a strong annual review process for all employees and executives. No one, not even a founder/CEO, is above a performance review. These can be shared by a board member or by the company's human resources executive. They don't have to be complicated. Just answer and discuss three questions: *What's working? What's not?* and *Where do we go from here?* Reviews are valuable in identifying blind spots, in exploring strengths and areas needing focus, and in creating a personal road map that aligns with your company's future.

Finally, as I've mentioned previously, every leader needs a strong leadership team around her to run and grow her business. These are people who will tell you what you *need* to hear, not what you *want* to hear. Flattery will get you nowhere, especially if you are an executive running a company. You must have people who will give it to you straight. It can take months and years to create that bond of trust, but with that in place, you certainly will be more attuned and receptive to their input.

REPLACING YOURSELF

Attending to succession improves the credibility and profitability profile of your enterprise. The deeper your bench, the more attractive your company will be to customers, to potential investors, to partners, and, yes, to acquisition prospects. Moreover, knowing that you have a potential successor in line can be very liberating for your own decision-making. Here are some tips when meeting and interviewing potential candidates:

- There are only two types of successors: those already inside your company and those who are outside, in the industry, whether working with a competitor, a partnering firm, or a related business. Evaluate candidates from all venues.

- Refrain from choosing someone who you think is just like you. People will only end up comparing them to you, which will be unproductive.

- Don't hire people from companies that are tremendously larger than yours or people who have never worked in a company of your current size. They will create policies and processes that don't fit and won't work for your business.

- Ask several people you trust and who are close to you, in addition to investors and board and/or advisory board members, to interview the candidates.

- When getting to know candidates, bring them outside the business setting to neutral ground. Make sure you can relate to each other over dinner or on a hike. Get to know them as human beings, not just as job candidates.

- Understand how they solve problems and mitigate risks. Ascertain whether they have experience solving the problems you know your company will face in the future.

- Get clarity around how they resolve conflict with others.

- Get a sense of how collaborative they are. Will they partner with you, seek and consider your opinion and advice, or will they disregard what you have built? Also, be very clear about your own intended level of involvement, and set expectations.

- Examine cultural and values fit.

As a founder/CEO, it can be difficult, even painful, to think about replacing yourself. Yet everyone is at some point replaceable. You are *in* business; you are not *the* business. Michelangelo created *David*, but he did not *become* that sculpture. He went on to paint the Sistine Chapel ceiling. Like Michelangelo, you the entrepreneur are free to attempt as many masterpieces as you want.

EXIT STRATEGIES AND TIMING

There are many different types of exits and many reasons you may sell, get acquired, or merge your business. Ideally, an exit strategy is the result of a plan developed and supported by you, your leadership team, your investors, and your board of directors. That plan can evolve over time and is implemented as and when the need or opportunity arises. For example, there may a lucrative opportunity to become strategically additive to another business, requiring transfer of ownership and job function. Conversely, your business may be pushing the limits of its model, so that selling while you still are on the upswing makes sense. In these examples, the nature of your company's exit strategy, combined with the interests of those who have majority control (which may still include you), help determine your role and function in the new entity.

Timing and foresight are crucially important in any exit. In my industry, for example, you sell your business and then go through an "earnout." That is, you get paid some money up front and then receive more payouts along the way, which are based on meeting certain performance metrics, such as retaining business and winning more of it.

In 95% of all businesses, you clearly want to avoid a sale before even the hint of an economic recession. But that still leaves some questions open. Is it better to sell when everything is going just great—when the market is up, demand is high, and your business is doing splendidly but also is clearly headed to even greater things? Or is it better to sell when you realize that the best you will ever attain is the number 2 or number 3 slot in your market? The answer to the first question could be "It's too soon," and the answer to the second might be "It's already too late." The actual answers lie in a very complicated mix of financial, market, competitive, and personal factors, of which you need to be ever mindful.

Still, there's nothing worse than missing the right opportunity because you had your blinders on. Waiting too long and being forced to sell an obsolete business in a shaky market when you've run out of gas is the worst possible outcome after years of slugging it out. The point is, you have to see the opportunities and market dynamics swirling around your business, but you also need to see them *early* enough to have sufficient runway to prepare for and deal with them properly.

As is too often the case, the moment you do realize you have a real opportunity to transact your business, you may not be ready to pull the trigger. Your numbers and your operation aren't optimized for a sale, and you haven't thought through what would go where or who would do what. You end up scrambling, feeling amateurish, putting a deal together that has not been completely thought through and that may not be entirely in your favor. Getting your business in shape for a transaction of any kind doesn't take a couple months. It can take years. In fact, you really should always be running your business as if you are preparing it for an exit.

THE MARATHON MINDSET

It may be counterintuitive and especially difficult for founder/CEOs to operate their businesses in perpetual anticipation of a sale. Yes, you absolutely want to focus on growing and running a solid business over the long term. But what if you did that with an eye toward transacting it? Business is all about change and transformation, not about eternity. Take care of your business today as if you were going to turn it over to someone else tomorrow. Wouldn't you want to leave it in the best possible condition? Wouldn't operating this way put you and your business in an optimal position?

I call this the marathon mindset. Running a business is a lot like running a marathon. There are grueling uphill parts, and flat, winding, and downhill parts. There are times when you're struggling to keep up and times when you're running at a good, steady pace. One way or the other, there is always a finish line. During the marathon, you are constantly monitoring your breathing, mind, pace, and fluid intake, aware of your environment and terrain, checking the time, thinking about that finish line. In business, the marathon mindset won't let you get too carried away or too comfortable. It will make you check on yourself and put you on your best, most ambitious behavior. As a result, you will run your business so much better and tighter. It will leave you being wanted rather than wanting, which is always the better position in a business transaction.

Put yourself in the shoes of a potential buyer or corporate CEO contemplating an acquisition. The first thing you will do is ponder your profitability with fresh, cold, critical eyes, spotting redundancies and inefficiencies with people and processes. You will probably look at your expenses first. Keep in mind, though, that your expenses are a finite proposition, and there is only so much belt tightening you can do. Expenses are important, but your revenues and potential new sources of income have a much more meaningful effect on the bottom line.

Expenses

What is the return on investment of your purchases, contracts, and agreements? Is there a way to consolidate certain functions to reduce expenses or to make them work harder for you? Take stock of your major business processes, audit them, and consider revisions and innovations in time, talent, and equipment requirements. What are the must-haves versus the nice-to-haves? Taking great care not to infringe upon your core values and culture, determine which benefits really matter. Are you compensating your best people well enough and putting poor performers on a plan? Cutting out the dead weight is not a once-every-couple-of-years kind of thing; you should be keeping an eye on it all the time.

Income
Look hardest at sales and business development. Is your market growing? Mature? Shrinking? What is the value of the companies with which you do business? What sales are you *not* capturing? Are there new competitors and technological advances on the horizon? Partners with whom you could expand your market and do revenue sharing? What are the key market trends? Economic conditions? Potential product line extensions? Are there vertical market opportunities? Look for trends, and plan accordingly. You want to be growing. Growth! The most attractive feature a potential buyer looks for is a future.

The marathon mindset is a state of being that will give your company the opportunity to operate at peak performance more consistently. It will get you outside of yourself and keep you on your toes while keeping you grounded. It also will keep your company healthy and toned, whether for a possible exit or to weather crises. The marathon mindset will crush the founder's curse—and by the way, it cannot be faked.

LIVING THE DREAM
I gave birth to my company before I gave birth to my children. Then I chose to put *my* name on the door, affirming that my baby was a total reflection of my identity, an image so hi-def that, for all practical purposes, it *was* my identity. I was the epitome of the typical founder/CEO: completely consumed with

my business, head full of steam, wired for sound, in the heart of Silicon Valley.

In the tech sector at that time, being an independent PR firm was a real drawing card. In fact, in the minds of our clients and our employees, the idea that we might sell, merge, or be acquired was viewed as almost undesirable. The change in service approach and culture that would come with a sale was considered far from a good thing, even though joining forces with a bigger firm could give us more breadth and depth. It was better to be the tony, untethered, independent firm that could turn on a dime for its clients and do what it wanted for its employees. Being independent was even in our mission statement. It was part of our brand.

I used to be very public, very vocal about how fiercely independent we were. I wouldn't even *discuss* an opportunity to merge with another firm, and I turned down what likely would have been several respectable and lucrative offers. Work for someone else? How could I? It would kill our culture, damaging our brand and everything we stood for.

For many years, this was a great thing. I ran my company this way and it worked, for the most part, for a long time. If I had to do it all over again, I still would turn down those offers. It was my choice, my desire, and I was *destined* to run my company (with all the leadership teams I had) for as long as I did. I was living the proverbial dream. It was a total blast, with only a few incredibly painful exceptions.

In the second half of its life, however, I might have run my firm differently. I had fallen prey to the founder's curse. The marathon mindset calls for envisioning a finish line. I didn't see a finish line because, well, for most of my company's existence, I didn't want one. (Until I did, that is.) I did not see that the greatest benefit of such a management approach would have been a more profitable and efficient business. This became more of an issue as our industry evolved, competition increased, and talent became extremely expensive, all of which squeezed our margins. When I was finally ready to think about selling my baby, it had become confused with my identity, and it was hard to face what it would take to get it ready.

PREPARE YOURSELF

While you need to prepare your business for sale or acquisition, you also need to prepare *yourself*. Being an entrepreneur or a founder/CEO is in your blood. Suddenly working inside someone else's company and "reporting" to someone can be an out-of-body experience. Finding yourself in an unfamiliar environment, with different people, doing potentially different work, is a sharp knock on the imposter syndrome's door.

When my company was acquired, part of me was proud and super motivated. *This is the next right step for me and my company and it's going to be great!* The other part of me was like, *Yikes! Who are all these people cc'd on my email and what do they expect of me?* I remember relying heavily on the guidance of my partners Brian Sinderson and Debra Raine, who had helped me get the firm in shape for a sale and had both worked for much larger firms before coming to work with me.

Even if you arrange it so that you are actually running your old company inside the new one, it will *not* be the same. Many of the people will be new to you, as will the ways of doing things. And the new ways won't just be new; they will be things that did not originate with you and that do not belong to you. Nevertheless, they are now yours to work with and to manage.

As I have noted, negotiating your own position inside New Company, if that is your desired plan, is as important as negotiating the financial terms of the deal. You will always be the founder of your company, but if you are acquired, you may no longer be its CEO. This is a different kind of lunar landscape. What exactly *are* you in charge of? What decision-making authority and control *do* you have?

In my case, I traded fiscal responsibility for an entrepreneurial business development role within the structure of Finn Partners, my acquirer, which was exactly what I wanted. I was (very) tired of running the day-to-day operations of a firm, but I still wanted to help build something and bring home the bacon. Peter Finn, the founder of Finn Partners and a trailblazer himself, knew what he was doing when he gave me and my company that opportunity. If you have been an entrepreneur for a long time, clinging onto the *right* degree of autonomy will soothe your soul.

For this same reason, take great care to see to it that the executives of your company are well taken care of and integrated into *their* transition. Understand clearly what the acquiring company is doing to assimilate and train your people. This includes being acutely aware of differences in HR policies, such as vacation and benefits. Some of these are terms that can be negotiated before your deal closes, and they go a long way toward setting the tone for a positive integration process.

If possible, try to take a break shortly after the completion of your deal. It's not a trivial exercise to sell your business and integrate with a new company. I was CEO of Horn Group on a Friday and the managing partner of Finn Partners' technology practice the following Monday. It was like finishing one twenty-four-year-long marathon and then starting a new one without resting up. It worked out fine, but I was emotionally and physically drained, which was a tough way to get started.

Seek like-minded people inside the new company. Find a mentor who has been through a similar transition. Then give yourself time and space to adjust. I suggest assigning a time horizon for evaluation, a date on which you will measure the success of the transaction—or the lack thereof.

THE FOUNDER'S BLESSING: MAKE IT, DON'T FAKE IT

All business—and all life, for that matter—is about change. Our task as humans is to navigate through that change to a successful outcome. In that sense, then, we are always in the process of "making it." That is the business of being alive. We are always searching, looking, and dreaming, whether for a better product, a new job, stronger health, deeper love, more money, a loftier title, or whatever. A better life. We identify these different goals in terms of "success."

In this book, I have shared what I have learned about achieving business success with integrity and running a company with no shortcuts. The lessons I learned arose from my own experiences and are born out of the mistakes I made as CEO of my own business while also addressing the challenges of our clients. I have covered how to become a leader on the job and how to build a team and a values-based culture and brand. Among other things, I have also discussed dealing with loneliness and have offered a quarter century of tips for running a smooth operation, winning (and coming back from losing), and managing crises. Finally, I have written about the challenges and rewards of selling the business you have created.

To the entrepreneur, founder, and CEO, being able to start, grow, and ultimately sell your business—profitably—is a huge measure of success. But here's the thing: it's *how* you achieve this success, the journey, that is its truest measure. The *how* is a collection of strategies, tactics, motives, and values that often are so incredibly hard to execute. They are intricately nuanced, and you certainly won't find them in any textbook. Doing it the right way, with integrity, evokes the pride and self-esteem that makes the success taste and smell so much sweeter.

In the process of making it, the entrepreneur learns enduring lessons. She realizes that she can face and stare down tremendous adversity without faking it—or even feeling the need to do so. Blessed with self-knowledge, she has endless passion to pursue new opportunities, to innovate and create new businesses. She will keep on learning and perfecting her approach along the way. She has the confidence to lead, to make her dreams come true, and to achieve success over and over again. She will make it because she knows there is simply no need to fake it. That is real leadership for real business success.

Ultimately, while this is a book about business mission, it is also about *life* mission. Trying to run a business with integrity is one dimension of how we should aspire to live our lives. How we enter and honor our relationships, treat others and ourselves, give and receive—these all are measures of life lived with integrity. It is, after all, the promise of a good life, of knowing, when your head hits the pillow each night, that you did everything you could that day in the best way possible. It is knowing that you did things right and did right by everybody else, too.

This is the definition of a successful life *and* a successful business. As business leaders, we serve a particular community, market, or industry. But we also have the opportunity to serve the world, leading both business and society by our example. This is worth striving for, keeping to, and, now more than ever, getting back to.

NOTES

Introduction

1. Securities and Exchange Commission v. Glenn W. Turner Enterprises, US Court of Appeals 474 F. 2d 476 (9th Cir. 1973), II, B.

2. Amy Cuddy, "Your Body Language May Shape Who You Are," TEDGlobal 2012 (June 2012), https://www.ted.com/talks/amy_cuddy_your_body_language_may_shape_who_you_are?language=en.

3. Dana Carney, "My Position on 'Power Poses,'" https://faculty.haas.berkeley.edu/dana_carney/pdf_My%20position%20on%20power%20poses.pdf.

Chapter One: Some Really Bad Advice

1. "Imposter Syndrome," *Psychology Today*, https://www.psychologytoday.com/us/basics/imposter-syndrome.

2. J. T. O'Donnell, "85 Percent of Job Applicants Lie on Resumes. Here's How to Spot a Dishonest Candidate," *Inc.*, August 15, 2017, https://www.inc.com/jt-odonnell/staggering-85-of-job-applicants-lying-on-resumes-.html.

3. The head-in-the-sand myth is a powerful metaphor, but to give actual ostriches their due, these fleet-footed animals respond to danger by outrunning almost any threat. They do dig holes to make nests or to find food, but when they gather in groups, some ostriches always stand guard, on the lookout for predators and other dangers.

4. Husson University Online, "Why Do People Lie? The Truth about Dishonesty," https://online.husson.edu/why-do-people-lie.

5. Lie Dharma Putra, "Fraudulently Misstating Financial Statements Methods," *Accounting Financial and Tax*, http://accounting-financial-tax.com/2010/02/fraudulently-misstating-financial-statements-methods.

6. Majority Staff of the Committee on Transportation and Infrastructure, *The Design, Development & Certification of the Boeing 737 Max*, Final Committee Report, September 2020, https://transportation.house.gov/imo/media/doc/2020.09.15%20FINAL%20737%20MAX%20Report%20for%20Public%20Release.pdf.

7. Benjamin Appelbaus, Davis S. Hilzenrath, and Amit R. Paley, "All Just One Big Lie," *Washington Post*, December 13, 2008, https://www.washingtonpost.com/wp-dyn/content/article/2008/12/12/AR2008121203970.html.

8. Carmen Nobel, "Bernie Madoff Explains Himself," *Working Knowledge*, October 24, 2016, https://hbswk.hbs.edu/item/bernie-madoff-explains-himself.

9. Martha Graybow, "Madoff Mysteries Remain as He Nears Guilty Plea," Reuters, March 11, 2009, https://www.reuters.com/article/topNews/ idUSTRE52A5JK20090311?pageNumber=2&virtualBrandChannel =0&sp=true.

10. John Carreyrou, "Hot Startup Theranos Has Struggled with Its Blood-Test Technology," *Wall Street Journal*, October 16, 2015, https://www.wsj.com/ articles/theranos-has-struggled-with-blood-tests-1444881901.

11. Taylor Dunn, Victoria Thompson, Rebecca Jarvis, and Ashleu Louszuko, "Ex-Theranos CEO Elizabeth Holmes Says 'I Don't Know' 600-Plus Times in Never-Before-Broadcast Deposition Tapes," ABC News, January 23, 2019, https://abcnews.go.com/Business/ theranos-ceo-elizabeth-holmes-600-times-broadcast-deposition/ story?id=60576630.

12. Leah Ginsberg and Tom Huddleston Jr., "The Psychology of Deception: How Elizabeth Holmes Fooled Everyone about Theranos for So Long," *MakeIt*, March 20, 2019, https://www.cnbc.com/2019/03/20/hbos-the-inventor-how -elizabeth-holmes-fooled-people-about-theranos.html.

Chapter Two: So You Want to Start a Company . . .

1. Weber Shandwick, "The CEO Reputation Premium: A New Era of Engagement," March 3, 2015, https://www.webershandwick.com/news/ the-ceo-reputation-premium-a-new-era-of-engagement.

Chapter Three: Becoming a CEO

1. Elena Lytkina Botelho, Kim Rosenkoetter Powell, Stephen Kincaid, and Dina Wang, "What Sets Successful CEOs Apart," *Harvard Business Review*, May–June 2017, https://hbr.org/2017/05/what-sets-successful-ceos-apart.

2. Botelho et al., "What Sets Successful CEOs Apart."

3. See G. H. Smart, "The CEO Genome," https://ceogenome.com/about.

Chapter Four: Becoming and Staying an Authentic Brand

1. Steve Andriole, "Forrester's 2020 Technology Predictions Are Right," *Forbes*, January 2, 2020, https://www.forbes.com/sites/steveandriole/2020/01/ 02/forresters-2020-business--technology-predictions-are-just-right/ #588109302f04.

2. See, for example, Vinnie Mirchandani, "Tech Marathoners: Sabrina Horn— Part 2," *Deal Architect*, July 3, 2018, https://dealarchitect.typepad.com/ deal_architect/2018/07/tech-marathoners-sabrina-hornpart-2.html.

3. Kasey Panetta, "8 Macro Factors That Will Shape the 2020s," *Smarter with Gartner*, July 27, 2020, https://www.gartner.com/smarterwithgartner/ 8-macro-factors-that-will-shape-the-2020s.

4. "The CEO Reputation Premium: Gaining Advantage in the Engagement Era," Weber Shandwick, https://www.webershandwick.com/uploads/news/files/ ceo-reputation-premium-infographic.pdf. Also see the 2017 Cohn & Wolfe Authentic Brands study, http://www.authentic100.com.

5. Johnson & Johnson, "Our Credo," https://www.jnj.com/credo.

6. "Budweiser 2017 Super Bowl Commercial: "Born the Hard Way," Budweiser Canada, https://www.youtube.com/watch?v=7ZmlRtpzwos; Monique Danao, "How Budweiser Maintains Itself as America's Best Beer Brand," *ReferralCandy* (blog), https://www.referralcandy.com/blog/budweiser-marketing-strategy.

7. Prologis, "Financial Highlights," https://ir.prologis.com/why-invest/why-invest/default.aspx From Corporate Overview as of December 31, 2020. Accessed February 3, 2021.

8. Mike Isaac, "Inside Uber's Aggressive, Unrestrained Workplace Culture," *New York Times*, February 22, 2017, https://www.nytimes.com/2017/02/22/technology/uber-workplace-culture.html; Polina Marinova, "Uber Exec Resigns after Sexual Harassment Allegations Surface from His Time at Google," *Fortune*, February 27, 2017, https://fortune.com/2017/02/27/uber-amit-singhal-resigns; Amir Efrati, "Uber Group's Visit to Seoul Escort Bar S parked HR Complaint," *The Information*, March 24, 2017, https://www.theinformation.com/articles/uber-groups-visit-to-seoul-escort-bar-sparked-hr-complaint; "Uber CEO Kalanick Argues with Driver over Falling Fares," *Bloomberg Quicktake*, February 28, 2017, https://www.youtube.com/watch?v=gTEDYCkNqns.

9. Russell Hotten, "Volkswagen: The Scandal Explained," BBC, December 10, 2015, https://www.bbc.com/news/business-34324772; Hiroko Tabuchi, Jack Ewing, and Matt Apuzzo, "6 Volkswagen Executives Charged as Company Pleads Guilty in Emissions Case," *New York Times*, January 11, 2017, https://www.nytimes.com/2017/01/11/business/volkswagen-diesel-vw-settlement-charges-criminal.html?_r=0; "Volkswagen's US Chief Leaves Troubled German Carmaker," BBC, March 9, 2016, https://www.bbc.com/news/business-35768912; David Shepardson, "US Indicts Six as Volkswagen Agrees to $4.3 Billion Diesel Settlement," Reuters, January 11, 2017, https://uk.reuters.com/article/us-volkswagen-emissions-epa/u-s-indicts-six-as-volkswagen-agrees-to-4-3-billion-diesel-settlement-idUKKBN14V1T0; Jack Ewing, "Ex-Volkswagen CEO Charged with Fraud over Diesel Emissions," *New York Times*, May 3, 2018, https://www.nytimes.com/2018/05/03/business/volkswagen-ceo-diesel-fraud.html; US Securities and Exchange Commission, "SEC Charges Volkswagen, Former CEO with Defrauding Bond Investors during 'Clean Diesel' Emissions Fraud," Litigation Release No. 24422, March 15, 2019, https://www.sec.gov/litigation/litreleases/2019/lr24422.htm.

10. Laura Stampler, "The 11 Worst Foreign Ad Translation Fails," *Business Insider*, May 17, 2012, https://www.businessinsider.com/worst-foreign-ad-translation-fails-2012-5; "17 Global Brand Failures and Some Hilarious Examples," https://www.linkedin.com/pulse/17-global-brand-failures-some-hilarious-examples-stefan-weynfeldt.

11. Ben Gilbert, "25 of the Biggest Failed Products from the World's Biggest Companies," *Business Insider*, October 17, 2019, https://markets .businessinsider.com/news/stocks/biggest-product-flops-in-history -2016-12-1023387040.

12. Tod Rafferty, "The Rise and Fall of Harley-Davidson Perfume," *RideApart*, June 6, 2017, https://www.rideapart.com/articles/253742/the-rise-and-fall -of-harley-davidson-perfume.

Chapter Five: Get Used to Lonely

1. Thomas J. Saporito, "It's Time to Acknowledge CEO Loneliness," *Harvard Business Review*, February 15, 2012, https://hbr.org/2012/02/ its-time-to-acknowledge-ceo-lo.

Chapter Six: *Leader* and *Loser* Both Begin with the Letter *L*

1. See the research data on resilient leadership reported in Joseph Folkman, "New Research: 7 Ways to Become a More Resilient Leader," *Forbes*, April 6, 2017, https://www.forbes.com/sites/joefolkman/2017/04/06/ new-research-7-ways-to-become-a-more-resilient-leader/#3994c0837a0c.

Chapter Eight: Way Off the Menu

1. See Ben Horowitz, *What You Do Is Who You Are: How to Create Your Business Culture* (New York: HarperBusiness, 2019), 234–238.

Chapter Nine: The Founder's Curse

1. Noam Wasserman, "The Founder's Dilemma," *Harvard Business Review*, February 2008, https://hbr.org/2008/02/the-founders-dilemma.

ACKNOWLEDGMENTS

Over the years, I've often been encouraged to write a book about my never dull, frequently crazy, always challenging, and fulfilling career as the founder and CEO of a public relations agency in the technology industry.

Well, here it is.

Above all else, *Make It, Don't Fake It* is about achieving business success with integrity. The backdrop—my profession, market focus, and experiences—is what brings this book to life so colorfully, earnestly, and sometimes painfully.

It is an account of the mistakes I made and lessons I learned, refracted through two lenses: that of running my own company and that of advising the executives of countless other companies for more than a quarter century. From both perspectives, this was always an exercise in uncovering, understanding, managing, and leading with the truth, as complex, harsh, and elusive as the truth can sometimes be. My purpose here is to encourage, advise, and guide leaders—whatever their calling or industry, and whether they are on the ascent or already in the top seat—to conduct themselves with integrity. Integrity is the ticket to success, and it is something to which we must urgently return.

In the process of writing this book, I'm grateful to have had the help of a ghostwriter, Alan Axelrod, a man as cool as his last name. It was a wonderfully collaborative effort, in which I gained more confidence with each chapter we iterated, found my voice, became a better writer, and was able to produce a book that I hope will inspire, help, and maybe even entertain its readers.

I owe a huge thanks to my literary agent, Jim Levine, for taking me on, and to the entire team at Berrett-Koehler for their support—specifically Neal Maillet, who found the "diamond in the rough" in my initial proposal; Anna Leinberger, who patiently guided me through the process; Valerie Caldwell and Susan Malikowski, for the cover design; Jeevan Sivasubramaniam, Kristen Frantz, and everyone in marketing and sales; as well as Steve Piersanti, Johanna Vondeling, and David Marshall, for their business vision. I'm so impressed with what the BK team is doing and the example they are setting for an industry in transition.

Special thanks to Fortier Public Relations and Weaving Influence for their support in the marketing and promotion of this book. It was wonderful sitting on the other side of *your* desks.

I want to extend a big thanks to Andy Cunningham, John Markoff, Geoffrey Moore, and Jennifer Brehl for sharing their insights about the very unique process of becoming a published author. And I would like to thank Diana Delaney, Leland Deane, and David Readerman for their input at various points, as well as Buck Canon, my favorite philosopher, for his critical insights throughout.

There is a cast of several thousand companies and their executive teams, journalists, analysts, venture capitalists, mentors, advisors, and special people with whom I've had the privilege to work and from whom I was so fortunate to learn over the course of my career. Most notably, these include the entire leadership team at PeopleSoft and at The Chasm Group, as well as Susan Chenoweth Beerman, Jack Bergen, Maureen Blanc, Helen Donnelly, Esther Dyson, Peter Finn, Giles Fraser, Jay Fulcher, Richard Funess, Ed Hanford, Bill Hewitt, Mark Hoffman, Matt Holleran, Judith Hurwitz, David Kirkpatrick, Beverly Lenihan, Otto Lerbinger, John Luongo, Darlene Mann, David Moore, Simone Otus, Eric Patterson, Mike Perlis, MR Rangaswami, Seth Rosenstein, Ray Rothrock, Darryl Salerno, Roger Sippl, Peter Sobiloff, Vicky Staveacre, Katey Watts, Ann Winblad, Sam Whitmore, and Bob Wright.

A heartfelt thanks to all 1,000+ of my employees, especially those on my extended leadership teams who were instrumental in driving my company, Horn Group, forward at various times during its twenty-four-year life span: Bryan Adams, Lisa Azizian, Ben Billingsley, Erin Brown, Todd Cadley, Marilyn Callaghan, Liza Colburn, Michelle Cox, Lauren Curley, Len Dieterle, Jessica Doehle, Alison Durant, Susan Etlinger, Ben Farrell, Dave Fausel, Garrett Fisher, Ed Garcia, Marsha Greeley, Nick Guarracino, Caroline Hacker, Gannon Hall, Bonnie Harris, Kelley Joyce, Angelle Kashanian, Jen Logan, Jaime Lovejoy Resmini, Dan Katzki, Kevin King, Gustavo Llamas, Letty Ledbetter, Annie Sun Mancuso, Mike Mancuso, Alison Marciano, Julian McBride, Erica McDonald, Barb McPherson, Dee Anna McPherson, Allyne Mills, Katey Mokelke, Brynn Moynihan, Kathleen O'Boyle, Erin O'Keeffe, Tim O'Keeffe, Elizabeth Orgel, Randy Orndorf, Vicky Paar, Nicole Pack, Gina Pacheco, Corie Pierce, Debra Raine, Paul Rakov, Barb Reichert, Shelley Risk, Carol Sato, Michelle Sieling, Annette Shimada, Katie Huang Shin, Brian Sinderson, Vitor Souza, Mara Stefan, Liz Stowasky, Jill Symon, Michael Teeling, Katie Uhlman, and Erin Zehr.

A special note of gratitude to Shannon Latta, who for almost twenty years helped me imagine, create, grow, navigate, fix, and reinvent so many aspects of the business, through multiple cycles of the economy, and the tech and PR industries we worked in. She did it all with style and grace, and she definitely never faked it.

To my parents, Dr. Christian F. Horn and Christa W. Horn: they gave me the tools, courage, and drive to believe in myself, to never give up, and to accomplish great things with hard work, integrity, humor, and generosity. And finally, to my incredible daughters, Grace and Christina, to whom I have dedicated this book: thank you for your encouragement throughout my entire writing journey. Mostly, though, you deserve a special shout-out for tolerating more than two decades of all my stories from work and the endless distractions, and for your constant support and understanding—then, now, and always. I'm infinitely proud of you, and hope I showed you that you, too, can achieve anything you want in life, with passion, dedication, and a straight arrow.

INDEX

A

accountability, 76, 135–138, 156
achievement, imposter syndrome in, 13
action bias in resilience, 133
adaptation to events, 102–103, 115, 118
   speed and flexibility in, 56–57
Adler, Alfred, 4, 5, 11, 12
advertising technology sector, 102, 142
advisory boards, 105–106
advisory groups, personal, 107
after-action evaluation, 135–136, 137–138,
   155–156
anxiety and stress of CEOs, 102–105
Apple, Inc., 73–74
authentic brands, 47, 69, 71–96
authentic leadership, 111–112, 118

B

benefits offered to employees, 81–82, 177
bias, gender-related, 67–69
Billingsley, Ben, 149
Blanc, Maureen, 39, 45
body language, 5, 164
Boeing, 25
brand creation and management, 35, 47, 69,
   71–96, 178
   carelessness in, 91
   and commoditization, 88–89
   consumer trust in, 73
   COVID-19 pandemic affecting, 72–73
   differentiation from competition in,
      93–94
   of enduring brands, 86–88
   fraud in, 90–91
   hype in, 19
   protection strategies in, 92–94
   in reality of change, 94–96
   reputation of CEO affecting, 73–74, 111
   strategy and tactics in, 118
Budweiser brand, 86–87
"build it and they will come" approach, 20–21
Busch, Adolphus, 87
business continuity plan after crisis, 146
business expansion and contraction
   brand protection in, 92–93
   consolidation of offices in, 102–103,
      124–126
   focus in, 118–121
   layoff decisions in, 24, 56, 83, 100
   leadership skills in, 167
   losses in, 137–139, 142–144
   marathon mindset in, 172–174, 175
   number of clients in, 42–44, 50, 51–52,
      119
   "peacetime" phase in, 65
   subcultures in, 93
   timing sale of business in, 171–172
   values in, 53, 76, 88, 92, 139
   "wartime" phase in, 65, 102–104, 115,
      150
business plan, 113–130
   adjustments to, 115
   on core values, 47–48
   for crisis, 145–146, 151–155
   execution of, 117–118, 119, 126–127
   on financial management, 41–42
   identifying missing elements of, 121–122
   for improvement after losses, 137–138
   interim, in difficult decisions, 110
   linear nature of, 122
   and Make It Happen box, 123–127
   realistic expectations in, 139–140
   for sale of business, 166–177
   strategies and tactics in, 117–118
   success defined in, 116–117
   for troubleshooting, 160–162
   value of, 115–116
   why question as starting point for, 116
business sale, planning for, 166–177
business start-up, 34–40, 48–50
   financial management plan in, 41–42
   founders in, 44–46. *See also* founders
   hiring decisions in, 40–41
   inspiration and motivation for, 32, 52
   rapid growth in, 42–44
   values in, 47–48, 75

C

Callaghan, Marilyn, 41, 43
Carney, Dana R., 5
Carreyrou, John, 27
change
   adaptation and flexibility in, 56–57,
      102–103, 115, 118
   brand management in, 94–96
   resilience in, 118
   stress and loneliness in, 102–104
   and succession planning, 166–177
chief executive officer (CEO). *See* leadership
child care issues, 103, 104, 108
clients
   in broad view of "whole" customer, 80
   collecting payments from, 42
   exceeding expectations of, 78–80
   in expansion of business, 42–44, 50,
      51–52, 119
   factors in selection of, 7, 43–44, 67, 68
   feedback from, 80
   first, fear in pitching to, 34–37
   inappropriate behavior of, 68–69, 82
   listening to, 93, 159
   responsibilities to company and, 113
   successful strategies for, 114
   trust in brand, 73
   value-added services for, 79
coaches, leadership, 106–107
Coca-Cola, 91
commoditization, 88–89
communication, 7, 56
   body language in, 5, 164
   in crisis management, 150, 151, 153,
      154, 156, 157
   in difficult conversations, 162–164
   listening in, 140–142, 159–160

"tell me more" as basis of, 140–141, 163
in trouble bubble, 161
compartmentalizing, 104, 113
  in crisis, 104, 129, 147, 154
  in Make It Happen box, 123, 124–125, 127
  in trouble bubble, 160
compensation of employees, 58–59, 112, 174, 177
competition, brand differentiation in, 93–94
complaints, listening to, 141–142, 159–160
confidence, 5, 12–14
  and arrogant lies in overconfidence, 22–23
  in decision making, 111
  loneliness affecting, 97
contingency plans in crisis, 145, 151–152, 155
conversations
  difficult, 162–164
  listening in, 140–142, 159–160
  silent periods in, 163
  "tell me more" as basis of, 140–141, 163
Cook, Tim, 73–74
Corporate Knights Global, 87
Cosmopolitan magazine, 91–92
Costner, Kevin, 20
COVID-19 pandemic, 72–73, 157–158
crisis management, 145–164, 178
  anxiety and stress in, 102–105
  categories of crises in, 147–148, 148f
  communication in, 150, 151, 153, 154, 156, 157
  compartmentalizing in, 104, 129, 147, 154
  in cumulative impact of everyday problems, 148, 158–160
  in employee fraud, 146–147, 148, 150–152, 155–156, 158
  in global pandemic, 157–158
  in Hurricane Sandy, 146–147, 148–150, 155, 156, 157
  plans for, 145–146, 151–155
  postmortem analysis of, 155–156
  rehearsal exercise on, 154
  vulnerability assessment in, 153
Cuddy, Amy, 5
culture, organizational, 3, 47–48, 71–96, 178

D

Dare to Be Great, 4
deception, 25, 26–28
decision making
  in authentic leadership, 111–112
  confidence in, 111
  on consolidation of offices, 102–103, 124–126
  in early adaptation, 56–57
  emotions affecting, 61, 126
  on employee compensation, 58–59, 112
  on employee layoffs, 24, 56, 83, 100
  identifying gaps in, 121–122
  inertia in, 109–110
  and learning to lead, 60–61
  loneliness in, 100–101
  Make It Happen box in, 123–129
  mistakes and poor results of, 132
  on-the-job training in, 58–59, 60

  pragmatism in, 61–62
  reality as basis of, 9, 24, 50
Deeter, Jessie, 28
depression, 102, 109
disaster recovery plan, 145–146
dressing for success, 13
Duffield, David, 33, 37, 87

E

Edison device, 27
education and training
  of CEOs, 58–60
  for employee professional development, 81
  values statement on, 76
efficiency measures affecting brand, 92
embezzlement, 146, 148, 150–152, 155–156, 158
emotions
  decisions based on, 61, 126
  in difficult conversations, 163
  exhaustion affecting, 134
  and loneliness of CEO, 98
  Make It Happen box approach to, 124, 147
  and necessary lies, 15
  and succession planning, 165–166, 174–176
empathy, and authentic brands, 72, 73
employees
  benefits offered to, 81–82, 177
  compensation of, 58–59, 112, 174, 177
  in expansion of business, 119
  as family, 77, 81, 83
  fraud and theft by, 146–147, 148, 150–152, 155–156, 158
  as friends, 100, 146, 150, 152
  gratitude for, 109
  hiring of. *See* hiring decisions
  inappropriate behavior of, 82
  layoff decisions concerning, 24, 56, 83, 100
  on leadership team, 63–64, 66
  matched to work, 123–124
  morale of, 93, 103
  performance review of, 80, 169
  professional development programs for, 81
  recognized for exceptional results, 80
  relationship with CEO, 98–100, 107, 152
  retention of, 81–82
  sale of business affecting, 177
enduring brands, 86–88
entrepreneurs, 178–179
  establishing company values, 47
  faking it by, 2, 3, 23
  founder role of, 45, 47
  inspiration and motivation for, 32
  loneliness of, 97–112
  risk management by, 38
  spirit of, 32, 37, 82
  succession planning by, 166–177
Environmental Protection Agency, 90–91
ethical issues in "acting as if," 14
exaggeration lies, 18–23
exit strategies and timing, 171–172

expectations
    of clients, values focused on, 78–80
    in crisis management, 157
    realistic, setting of, 139–140

F

fabrication lies, 26
failures and losses, 131–144. *See also* losses and
    failures
"fake it till you make it," 1, 2, 4–5
    authentic leadership compared to, 111
    and limits to knowledge, 140
    on-the-job training compared to, 60
Fake-O-Meter, 11, 12f
faking it, 1–2, 3, 140
    and "acting as if," 4–5, 13–14, 15, 48
    authentic leadership compared to, 111
    as bad advice, 28
    in business start-up, 48–50
    continuum of lies in, 11–28
    and limits to knowledge, 140
    on-the-job training compared to, 60
    origin of, 4–5
family
    employees as, 77, 81, 83
    and work–life balance, 107–108
family-owned businesses, 87–88
fears in business start-up, 34–40, 48–50
financial issues
    in business start-up plan, 41–42
    in employee compensation, 58–59, 112
    in employee layoffs, 24, 56, 83
    marathon mindset approach to,
        173–174
    pragmatic approach to, 61–62
    stress and loneliness in decisions on, 103
financial recession (2008), 102, 118, 157
Finn Partners, 8, 82, 177
Forrester Research, 72
Founder Institute, 106
founders, 165–179
    and company value system, 47–48, 75
    loneliness of, 97–112
    roles and responsibilities of, 44–46
    succession planning by, 166–177
founder's blessing, 178–179
founder's curse, 165–179
The Founder's Dilemmas (Wasserman), 166
fraud
    in employee embezzlement, 146–147,
        148, 150–152, 155–156, 158
    in product promotion, 90–91
friends
    in business network, 101, 106, 149, 155
    employees as, 100, 146, 150, 152
future of company, vision of, 54, 63
    in long-term view, 120, 153
    statement on, 84–86
    strategy based on, 117, 118
    and succession planning, 164, 166–177
    values-driven, 89

G

Gartner Group, 73
gaslighting, 26
Gates, Bill, 37

gender of CEO, 66–69
    and loneliness, 98
    stereotypes of, 59
    and work–life balance, 107–108
gig workers, 90
gratitude, 109
Greenspan, Alan, 20
Grove, Andy, 65

H

halo effect, 78, 83
Hamburger Helper solution, 44
Harley-Davidson, 92
Harvard Business Review, 97, 98
hiring decisions, 40–41
    for leadership team, 63–64, 66
    in succession planning, 169–171
Hitler, Adolf, 90
Holmes, Elizabeth, 2, 27–28, 91
Horn Group, 6, 8, 52, 177
Horowitz, Ben, 47
humility, 55, 62–63
Hurricane Sandy, 146–147, 148–150, 155,
    156, 157

I

IBM, 133–136
identity of founders, 165–166, 174–176
imposter syndrome, 13, 50, 97, 176
inappropriate behavior, 68–69, 82
income, in marathon mindset, 174
integrity, 3, 9, 178, 179
    leading with, 54–55
    in losses and failures, 136, 137
    values statement on, 76–77
Intel Corporation, 65
interviews
    with clients, 75
    exaggeration lies in, 18–19
    with potential successors, 170
isolation and loneliness, 97–112

J

Jobs, Steve, 73–74
Johnson, Robert Wood, 84
Johnson & Johnson, 84–86
Jordan, Wilma, 149

K

Kalanick, Travis, 90
knowledge
    humility about, 55, 62–63
    and intuition, 57
    limits of, 140
    from listening to others, 140–141

L

Latta, Shannon, 94, 127
layoff decisions, 24, 56, 83, 100
leadership, 28–29, 50, 51–53
    annual performance review of, 169
    authentic, 111–112, 118
    brand management by, 71–96, 111
    commitment of, 56
    communication skills of, 7, 56, 140–141
    crisis management by, 145–164
    employee layoff decisions of, 24

flexibility and adaptation of, 56–57
focus of, 118–121
future vision of, 54, 63
gender of, 59, 66–69, 98, 107–108
humility of, 55, 62–63
integrity of, 54–55
learning to lead, 60–61
loneliness of, 97–112
losses and failures of, 131–144
missing elements identified by, 121–122
in New Company, 176–177
on-the-job training of, 58–60
optimism of, 54, 110
personality characteristics of, 53–58
reality-based. *See* reality-based leadership
relationship with employees, 98–100,
    107, 152
reputation of, 73–74, 111
resilience of, 55–56, 121, 132–133
responsibility to company and clients, 113
stereotypes on, 59
strategy and tactics of, 117–118
stress and anxiety of, 102–105
succession planning, 166–177
team in support of. *See* leadership team
values and standards modeled by, 48, 75
leadership team, 63–64, 66, 129–130
    as circle or bubble, 105
    in decision-making, 100, 101
    disagreements with, 130
    member characteristics in, 63–64, 66
    monthly meetings of, 83
    trust in, 169
learning, 58–63, 139
    from failures and losses, 137–139,
        143–144
legitimacy of leadership, 53
Lerbinger, Otto, 6
lies, continuum of, 11–28
listening
    to clients, 93, 159
    to complaints, 141–142, 159–160
    to "tell me more," 140–141, 163
loneliness, 97–112, 178
long-term view, 120, 153, 172–174, 175
losses and failures, 131–144
    in business cycles, 142–144
    communication and listening in,
        140–142
    in IBM account, 133–136
    integrity and accountability in, 135–138
    learning from, 137–139, 143–144
    plan for improvement in, 137–138
    postmortem evaluation of, 135–136,
        137–138
    and realistic expectations, 139–140
    resilience in, 132–133
Lotus software company, 36
luck, 32

M
MacNiven, Jamis, 88
Madoff, Bernie, 2, 26–27, 28
Make It Happen box, 123–129, 147
Mancuso, Mike, 104
market value, 20, 47, 73–74

McGlinchey, Dick, 36
McPherson, Dee Anna, 102
"meaningful time," 109
meetings, 78–79
    of leadership team, 83
    with peer groups, 106
    with self, for thinking time, 110–111
mentors, 106–107, 109, 177
minimization lies, 24–25
mission of company, 84–86, 117, 118, 175
    and life mission, 179
mistakes, losses and failures in, 131–144
Moghadam., Hamid R., 87
Moore, Dave, 149
morale of employees, 93, 103
motivation
    in business start-up, 32, 52
    in continuum of lies, 28
    organizational culture affecting, 81
    values statement on, 76
multitasking, 122–129, 147, 154

N
Norwest Venture Partners, 33

O
Olympics Information Systems, 133–136
omission lies, 25
Only the Paranoid Survive (Grove), 65
on-the-job training, 58–60
opportunities, recognition of, 119–121
optimism, 54, 110, 155
Orbitz, 95
Orgel, Elizabeth, 134, 136
Otus, Simone, 39, 45
overconfident and arrogant lies, 22–23

P
Pacheco, Gina, 132
parallel processing, 123, 126–127, 128
P.C. Richard & Son, 87–88
"peacetime" phase of business, 65
peer groups, 106
people-related problems, 162
PeopleSoft, 33–37, 42–43, 87
performance review
    annual, 169
    client satisfaction as factor in, 80
    on crisis management, 155–156
    in losses and failures, 135–136, 137–138
    in successes, 136
Perlis, Mike, 146, 147, 150
personality characteristics
    of leader, 53–58
    of leadership team members, 63–64
personal relationships
    in business network, 101, 106, 149, 155
    C-level title affecting, 98
    with employees, 100, 146, 150, 152
    stress of new venture affecting, 38
    tall tales for impression in, 17–18
Petopia.com, 21
Pets.com, 21
pitching for new accounts, 33–37, 133–136
Ponzi schemes, 2, 26
postmortem analysis, 135–136, 137–138,
    155–156

posture, and self-confidence, 5
pragmatism, 61–62, 110
Premier smokeless cigarette, 91
pretending, therapeutic use of, 4, 12–14
problem solving, 148, 158–164
    in failures and losses, 137–139, 140–141,
        143–144
    Make It Happen box in, 123–129
    "tell me more" conversations in,
        140–141, 163
    troubleshooting in, 78, 160–162
Prologis, 87
Puffs toilet tissue, 91
pyramid schemes, 4

Q

quiet times, insight in, 110–111

R

Raine, Debra, 162, 176
reality-based leadership, 9, 54, 69, 71
    adaptation and flexibility in, 57
    brand authenticity in, 71–96
    in business growth and expansion, 50
    in business start-up, 36, 42, 45, 46
    decision-making in, 9, 24, 50
    in founder role, 45
    future vision in, 54, 63
    humility in, 55
    and imposter syndrome, 13, 50
    integrity in, 3, 55
    optimism in, 54
    ostrich lies in avoidance of, 23–24
    strategy and tactics in, 118
    team members in, 63
Regina vacuum cleaners, 25
resilience, 132–133
    and commitment, 55–56
    and focus, 121
    in strategy and tactics, 118
responsibility
    to company and clients, 113
    for losses and failures, 137–138
    and minimization lies, 24–25
retention of employees, 81–82
Richard, Pieter Christian, 88
risk management, 38–40, 48–50
R.J. Reynolds Tobacco Company, 91

S

Sabrina Horn Public Relations, 33, 34, 52
sale of business, planning for, 166–177
Salerno, Darryl, 150
Samsung smartphones, 91
S corporation, organization as, 8, 42, 52
setbacks, resilience in, 55–56, 132–133
Shimada, Annette, 41
short-term view, 120, 153
Sinderson, Brian, 176
Sinek, Simon, 116
sole proprietorship, 42
Soltes, Eugene, 26
Start with Why (Sinek), 116
Stefan, Mara, 102
stereotype of CEOs, 59

strategy, 117–118, 120, 125–126
    for exit, 171–172
stress and anxiety of CEOs, 102–105
success, 114
    after-action evaluation of, 136
    criteria and measures of, 116–117,
        178, 179
succession planning, 164, 165–177
Sullivan, Jeanne, 149
support system for CEOs, 105–107
survival instincts, 31–32, 50

T

tactics, 117–118, 126–127
team approach, 76, 78
    leadership team in. *See* leadership team
Teeling, Mike, 82
Theranos, 2, 27–28, 91
Tillich, Paul, 110
time management, 107–109, 110–111
troubleshooting, 78, 160–162
trust of consumers in brand, 73
truth telling, 25, 35–36
Turner, Glenn W., 4

U

Uber, 90

V

value-added services, 79
values, 178
    in brand management, 3, 47, 69, 71–96,
        178
    in business expansion and contraction,
        53, 76, 88, 92, 139
    at founding, 47–48, 75
    in inappropriate behavior, 68–69
    statement of, 75, 76–78, 84–86
    strategy based on, 114, 117, 118
    vision for company based on, 89
van der Rohe, Mies, 116–117
Vistage, 106
visualization strategies, 13
VoicePower, 82
Volkswagen, 90–91
vulnerability assessment in crisis plan, 153

W

"wartime" phase of business, 65, 102–104,
    115, 150
Wasserman, Noam, 166
Weber Shandwick public relations firm, 73
What You Do Is Who You Are: How to Create Your
    Business Culture (Horowitz), 47
white lies, 14–15
winging it, 18
Winterkorn, Martin, 91
women as CEOs, 66–69, 98, 107–108
World Trade Center attack, 157

Y

Young Presidents' Organization, 106

Z

Zecher, Linda, 36

ABOUT THE AUTHOR

S abrina Horn is an award-winning CEO, communications expert, advisor, and author. She founded Horn Group, a public relations firm, with $500 and five years' job experience, becoming one of few female CEOs in Silicon Valley in the early 1990s. Over a quarter century, her firm advised thousands of executives and their companies—from the hottest start-ups to the Fortune 500—doing so with a special focus on authenticity.

As a young executive, Horn learned about leadership through two lenses: one, as CEO growing and running her firm, the other, as strategic advisor guiding her clients through their own unique business challenges. Facing countless difficult situations, crises, even failure, she came to understand that leadership is about making the right decisions at the right time based on the often very harsh realities of the truth. Through her journey, she learned that there are no short cuts to achieving long-term business success. Still, she confesses to having made many mistakes, and now in her first book, she shares what she learned about how to make it without faking it.

Horn Group became one of the most enduring, iconic brands in the tech world, with multiple offices in the US and global reach. It received national acclaim as best US employer, best US tech agency, and as a top 10 US independent tech PR firm, among many other accolades for excellence in service and creativity. In 2015, Horn oversaw her firm's successful acquisition by Finn Partners, a global marketing company.

Today, Horn is CEO of HORN Strategy, LLC, a consultancy focused on helping entrepreneurs and CEOs navigate the early stages of their businesses. She serves as an advisor and board member for a number of organizations and is a frequent speaker at industry forums and leadership conferences.

Born in 1961, Horn is the only child of German immigrants, both survivors of the infamous fire bombings of Dresden in WWII. She has a BA in American studies from Hobart and William Smith Colleges, and an MS in public relations from Boston University. She has two daughters, Grace and Christina, two extremely large goldendoodles, and splits her time between New York and San Francisco.

HORN
STRATEGY

ABOUT HORN STRATEGY, LLC

HORN Strategy is a consulting firm focused on helping entrepreneurs and CEOs build and lead their emerging businesses.

Established by Sabrina Horn in 2020, Horn works directly with executives, providing guidance on when and how to raise capital, go-to-market strategies, brand building, and market expansion. Horn offers keen insights on how to clearly communicate critical messages to different audiences and provides crisis counsel. Strategic connections and access to funding, marketing, professional services, executive coaching and mentoring are also a vital part of Horn's practice.

Sabrina Horn is a frequent speaker at industry conferences and forums on a broad range of topics about leadership, entrepreneurship, problem-solving, and creating success. Learn more at www.sabrinahorn.com.

 **Berrett–Koehler**
Publishers

Berrett-Koehler is an independent publisher dedicated to an ambitious mission: *Connecting people and ideas to create a world that works for all.*

Our publications span many formats, including print, digital, audio, and video. We also offer online resources, training, and gatherings. And we will continue expanding our products and services to advance our mission.

We believe that the solutions to the world's problems will come from all of us, working at all levels: in our society, in our organizations, and in our own lives. Our publications and resources offer pathways to creating a more just, equitable, and sustainable society. They help people make their organizations more humane, democratic, diverse, and effective (and we don't think there's any contradiction there). And they guide people in creating positive change in their own lives and aligning their personal practices with their aspirations for a better world.

And we strive to practice what we preach through what we call "The BK Way." At the core of this approach is *stewardship,* a deep sense of responsibility to administer the company for the benefit of all of our stakeholder groups, including authors, customers, employees, investors, service providers, sales partners, and the communities and environment around us. Everything we do is built around stewardship and our other core values of *quality, partnership, inclusion,* and *sustainability.*

This is why Berrett-Koehler is the first book publishing company to be both a B Corporation (a rigorous certification) and a benefit corporation (a for-profit legal status), which together require us to adhere to the highest standards for corporate, social, and environmental performance. And it is why we have instituted many pioneering practices (which you can learn about at www.bkconnection.com), including the Berrett-Koehler Constitution, the Bill of Rights and Responsibilities for BK Authors, and our unique Author Days.

We are grateful to our readers, authors, and other friends who are supporting our mission. We ask you to share with us examples of how BK publications and resources are making a difference in your lives, organizations, and communities at www.bkconnection.com/impact.

Dear reader,

Thank you for picking up this book and welcome to the worldwide BK community! You're joining a special group of people who have come together to create positive change in their lives, organizations, and communities.

What's BK all about?

Our mission is to connect people and ideas to create a world that works for all.

Why? Our communities, organizations, and lives get bogged down by old paradigms of self-interest, exclusion, hierarchy, and privilege. But we believe that can change. That's why we seek the leading experts on these challenges—and share their actionable ideas with you.

A welcome gift

To help you get started, we'd like to offer you a **free copy** of one of our bestselling ebooks:

www.bkconnection.com/welcome

When you claim your **free ebook**, you'll also be subscribed to our blog.

Our freshest insights

Access the best new tools and ideas for leaders at all levels on our blog at ideas.bkconnection.com.

Sincerely,

Your friends at Berrett-Koehler